VSEVOLOD MEYERHOLD

Routledge Performance Practitioners is a series of introductory guides to the key theatre-makers of the last century. Each volume explains the background to and the work of one of the major influences on twentieth- and twenty-first-century performance.

These compact, well-illustrated and clearly written books will unravel the contribution of modern theatre's most charismatic innovators. *Vsevolod Meyerhold* is the first book to combine:

- a biographical introduction to Meyerhold's life
- a clear explanation of his theoretical writings
- an analysis of his masterpiece production *Revisor, or The Government Inspector*
- a comprehensive and usable description of the 'biomechanical' exercises he developed for training the actor.

As a first step towards critical understanding, and as an initial exploration before going on to further, primary research, **Routledge Performance Practitioners** are unbeatable value for today's student.

Jonathan Pitches is a Principal Lecturer in Performing Arts at Manchester Metropolitan University. He has taught Russian acting techniques, including biomechanics, for many years and has written extensively on Russian theatre and the relationship between training and performance.

ROUTLEDGE PERFORMANCE PRACTITIONERS

Series editor: Franc Chamberlain, University College Northampton

Routledge Performance Practitioners is an innovative series of introductory handbooks on key figures in twentieth-century performance practice. Each volume focuses on a theatre-maker whose practical and theoretical work has in some way transformed the way we understand theatre and performance. The books are carefully structured to enable the reader to gain a good grasp of the fundamental elements underpinning each practitioner's work. They will provide an inspiring springboard for future study, unpacking and explaining what can initially seem daunting.

The main sections of each book will cover:

*   personal biography
*   explanation of key writings
*   description of significant productions
*   reproduction of practical exercises.

The first volumes of the series are:

Michael Chekhov by Franc Chamberlain
Jacques Lecoq by Simon Murray
Vsevolod Meyerhold by Jonathan Pitches
Konstantin Stanislavsky by Bella Merlin

Future volumes will include:

Eugenio Barba
Pina Bausch
Augusto Boal
Bertolt Brecht
Peter Brook
Jerzy Grotowski
Anna Halprin
Joan Littlewood
Ariane Mnouchkine

VSEVOLOD
MEYERHOLD

Jonathan Pitches

LONDON AND NEW YORK

First published 2003
by Routledge
11 New Fetter Lane, London EC4P 4EE

Simultaneously published in the USA and Canada
by Routledge
29 West 35th Street, New York, NY 10001

Routledge is an imprint of the Taylor & Francis Group

Typeset in Perpetua by
Florence Production Ltd, Stoodleigh, Devon
Printed and bound in Great Britain by
TJ International Ltd, Padstow, Cornwall

British Library Cataloguing in Publication Data
A catalogue record for this book is available from
the British Library

Library of Congress Cataloging in Publication Data
Pitches, Jonathan, 1968–
    Vsevolod Meyerhold/Jonathan Pitches.
       p. cm. – (Routledge performance practitioners)
    Includes bibliographical references and index.
    1. Meyerhold, V.E. (Vsevolod Emilevich), 1874–1940.   2. Theatrical
    producers and directors – Soviet Union – Biography.   I. Title.
    II. Series.
    PN2728.M4P58 2003
    792′.0233′092 – dc21   2003003595

ISBN 0–415–25883–9 (hbk)
ISBN 0–415–25884–7 (pbk)

TO CERI, HARRI AND GEORGE

It's very important in biomechanics that you're working with very simple things, very simple movements. You put them together and you can make something very complicated. But they are, in essence, simple.

(Aleksei Levinski, 1995)

CONTENTS

List of figures   **ix**

Acknowledgements   **xi**

1   A LIFE OF CONTRADICTIONS   **1**

     Apprenticeship (1874–1905) 4

     St Petersburg (1906–17) 12

     Meyerhold and the Revolution (1917–22) 29

     The Meyerhold Theatre (1922–31) 37

     The death of Meyerhold and his theatre (1932–40) 39

     Meyerhold today 42

2   MEYERHOLD'S KEY WRITINGS   **43**

     Don't (always) believe what you read! 43

     The key theoretical principles 46

     Naturalism 47

     Stylisation 50

     Rhythm and music 53

     The mask 57

     The grotesque 61

     Biomechanics and the actor of the future 67

     Chaplin and Eisenstein: a theory of montage 73

3 **MEYERHOLD'S KEY PRODUCTION:** *THE GOVERNMENT INSPECTOR*   77

    Gogol's challenge 77
    Meyerhold's response 78
    Nikolai Gogol: the comet 81
    Gogol's *Government Inspector* 83
    Meyerhold's *Government Inspector* 89

4 **PRACTICAL EXERCISES**   111

    Practice: the living link with Meyerhold 111
    So what *are* the basic skills of a biomechanical actor? 112
    The exercises 117
    Skills-based exercises 120
    Back to the basic skills 142
    Improvisation exercises 144
    Work on text 150
    Conclusions 153

Bibliography   155

    Books and articles 155
    Films and videos 158

Index   159

FIGURES

1.1 Portrait of the young Meyerhold, 1898   7

1.2 *Sister Beatrice*, 1906   15

1.3 Grigoriev's portrait of Dr Dapertutto, 1916   24

1.4 *Masquerade* at the Aleksandrinsky, 1917   28

1.5 Meyerhold the Bolshevik, 1922   31

1.6 Model reconstruction of *The Magnanimous Cuckold*, 1922   35

1.7 Three actors in *The Magnanimous Cuckold*, 1922   36

1.8 Meyerhold, 1932   40

2.1 Francisco Goya's *The Sleep of Reason Produces Monsters*, 1797   66

3.1 Meyerhold's *Government Inspector*: 'Dumbshow', 1926   80

3.2 Meyerhold's *Government Inspector*: 'Bribes', 1926   94

3.3 Meyerhold's *Government Inspector*: 'Reading the letter', 1926   107

4.1–4.20 The actions of the étude 'The Slap', 2002   128–37

ACKNOWLEDGEMENTS

I am indebted to the following people in offering support and help in the production of this book. First, I must give thanks to all my students, past and present, who have worked with me in the studio on biomechanics, especially to Lorna Wood and Mike Hayhurst. Second, I would like to thank my colleagues at University College Northampton, with whom I have spent countless hours discussing the Russian tradition of acting. Third, I am very grateful for the technical support of Carl Kirk and Tim Halliday. I am also indebted to Frances Carlyon at the Bristol Theatre Collection; Teresa Vargas at the Goya Museum in Madrid; and Robert Leach and Edward Braun for permission to reproduce photographic material. In addition, my thanks must go to Talia Rodgers and to Franc Chamberlain for their enthusiasm and encouragement. Finally, I would like to express my deepest gratitude to my family, especially my wife, Ceri, for giving me the time to write this book.

A LIFE OF
CONTRADICTIONS

Meyerhold's life was abruptly brought to an end in the basement of a prison in Moscow over sixty years ago. He was an old man, nearing his seventies, and had dedicated over two-thirds of his life to the Russian theatre, much of it to the cause of Communism after the Russian Revolution in 1917. After a life-long career of innovation and experiment his presence as a theatrical figurehead was deemed too dangerous by the Soviet authorities. He was tortured, 'persuaded' to confess to charges of spying and finally shot, a little less than a week after his sixty-sixth birthday.

It was the last of many contradictions in Meyerhold's life. From his theatrical theories to his relationships with others, Meyerhold courted controversy, even to the extent of promoting dissent among his audiences:

> If everyone praises your production, almost certainly it is rubbish. If everyone abuses it, then perhaps there is something in it. But if some praise and others abuse, if you can split the audience in half, then for sure it is a good production.

> (Gladkov 1997: 165)

His was a theatre based expressly *on* contradiction, a theatre which strove not to smooth out problems or to resolve paradoxes but to let them resonate within the minds of his performers and his audiences. A divided audience, Meyerhold argued, was more likely to engage at a deeper level with the content of the production, to turn in on itself, discuss and debate. We have all travelled back from the theatre with friends and talked about the spectacle we have just enjoyed. But how much more lively is the discussion if, for some reason, we don't agree on everything we have seen? This was Meyerhold's logic and it informed much of his practice.

There were contradictions in Meyerhold's life as well. Often labelled an opponent of Stanislavsky's, he ended his career holding the reins of his teacher's last directorial project, described by the dying Stanislavsky as his 'sole heir in the theatre' (Benedetti 1990: 345). Although he was reputed to be a dictator and a control freak, Meyerhold's workshop nevertheless produced a startling range of theatrical freethinkers, each one capable of enriching the Russian tradition in their own right. Notorious for being difficult to work with, his record of collaboration with musicians, artists, playwrights and co-directors belies this image, and instead defines a man with an irrepressible desire to move with the times and to learn from the people who defined those times.

Meyerhold undoubtedly manufactured some of this controversy, but the one contradiction over which he had no control was his relationship with the political powers of Soviet Russia. He was overtly supportive of the new powers from the earliest opportunity and much of his work in the early 1920s was geared to furthering the cause of the new Soviet regime. It is difficult to believe, then, that those who embraced Meyerhold's vitality in the early years of the Revolution were also responsible for extinguishing it. But this was precisely what happened. It may have taken over twenty years for the turn-around to be completed but its conclusion was undeniably decisive. What is more, Meyerhold's fate was anything but unique. He was joining a long roll-call of artists whose love of experimentation finally became an unendurable threat to the leader of the Soviet Union, Joseph Stalin.

But why begin here, at the end of Meyerhold's story, rather than at the beginning? First, because Meyerhold's death offers us a measure of how seriously the authorities in the Soviet Union (and before the Revolution, under the Tsar) viewed the art of the theatre. British politicians no longer see the theatre as posing a threat to their authority, and the fact that people might be killed in order to silence its voice is almost incomprehensible to us today. But in the post-revolutionary climate of the new Soviet Union, live theatre was viewed as one of the most effective tools of communication – not least because most of its audiences were unable to read. To be in control of this weapon of communication gave the director great power, but it was power that came at a cost and for many Soviet artists the weapon proved double-edged.

Second, by reversing the chronology of his story, we are recognising that any version of Meyerhold's life is somehow uncontrollably coloured by his death. The bitter irony of his demise hangs over his work, constantly reminding us of the volatile context within which he was practising his art. In a way, this foreknowledge captures the kind of attitude Meyerhold himself wanted to inculcate in his audiences. He, like Bertolt Brecht, did not want his spectators to focus their 'eyes on the finish' (Brecht 1978: 37), but instead to engage in the material of the production in a consciously enquiring manner. For this reason, Meyerhold delighted in revealing the mechanics of the theatre. He filled his productions with self-conscious theatricalities, arranging the order of the scenes in such a way that they might collide against one another rather than seamlessly fuse together. We might conclude from this that, in Meyerhold's thinking, people's lives are similarly unpredictable. They do not unfold in a smooth, organised way (as the naturalistic repertoire often suggested), but are multifaceted, problematic and surprising. In Meyerhold's own case this could not have been more true.

So, with our eyes diverted from the finish and focused now on the course, let us examine the episodes of Meyerhold's life, from his early years before he met Stanislavsky to the final period of his career before his arrest by the NKVD (the no-less-brutal predecessors of the KGB). We will cover the following ground:

- Apprenticeship (1874–1905)
- St Petersburg (1906–17)
- Meyerhold and the Revolution (1917–22)
- The Meyerhold Theatre (1922–31)
- The death of Meyerhold and his theatre (1932–40)
- Meyerhold today.

APPRENTICESHIP (1874–1905)

LIFE BEFORE THE MOSCOW ART THEATRE

As the eighth child of the family, Vsevolod Meyerhold had to work hard to make an impression. He was born into the affluent family of the German vodka distiller, Emil Meyerhold, on 28 January 1874, and, recognising that he would never inherit the family business, he developed a much closer relationship with his mother, Alvina, than with his businessman father. At such a distance from the head of the family, the young Meyerhold did not find himself obliged to espouse all of his father's values. Instead, he mixed with the workers from the distillery and attended music concerts and the theatre. The artistic influence was so great that at the age of nineteen he was already able to define his career path, claiming an even earlier calling in his diary:

> I have talent, I know that I am a good actor. . . . This is my most cherished dream, one I have thought about almost since I was five.
>
> (Gladkov 1997: 4)

But the decision to enter the theatre wasn't as clear cut as it might have seemed. Two alternative careers presented themselves to Meyerhold – one as a lawyer, the other as a violinist. In fact, it was the former occupation which first beckoned him and which provided his escape route from the provincial town of Penza to the bustling city of Moscow. Meyerhold began reading for a degree in law at Moscow University in 1895, after graduating with some effort from his school in Penza. Once in Moscow he faced what he called 'a crossroads' in his life (Gladkov 1997: 91), torn by the equally appealing possibilities of a theatre training or a career as a second violinist in the University orchestra. Failing the orchestra's audition made the decision not to play 'second fiddle' unnecessary and instead, in 1896, he went into two years of actor training with the playwright and director Vladimir Nemirovich-Danchenko at the Moscow Philharmonic school. Music continued to play a significant part in Meyerhold's career, however, and although he gave up the violin and later looked back at his failure with some relief, he never turned his back on the discipline of music itself. Indeed, the *musicality* of many of his productions is a notable characteristic of his directorial approach.

VLADIMIR NEMIROVICH-DANCHENKO AND KONSTANTIN STANISLAVSKY

Nemirovich-Danchenko is best known for his stormy relationship with the director Konstantin Stanislavsky and for co-founding the Moscow Art Theatre (MAT) with him, arguably the most famous theatre in all of Russia. But before he began this collaboration with Stanislavsky in 1898, Nemirovich had already established a well-earned reputation as a creative artist and, if anything, it was he who was the most experienced theatre professional in the early days of the MAT. For his part, Stanislavsky had begun cutting his teeth as an actor and a director ten years earlier at the semi-professional dramatic society known as the Alexeiev Circle. There, he developed an impressive range of character roles, many of which were revived under the auspices of the MAT.

Nemirovich was not an actor. Essentially he was a literary man with an intuitive eye for great writing. It was he, for example, who first recognised the dramatic talent of Anton Chekhov, calling for *The Seagull* (1896) to be awarded the Griboedov literary prize in place of his own play: *The Worth of Life* (1896). But although his talents lay first and foremost with the dramatic text, he also had experience as a director and, judging by the range of activities he lists in his autobiography, was clearly interested in teaching too. Meyerhold's tuition, he tells us, 'went far beyond the bounds of first experiments in stage technique'. It also involved:

> Psychological movements, everyday features, moral questions, emotional mergings with the author, aspirations towards frankness and simplicity, the quest of vivid expression and diction, mimicry, plastics, self-assurance.
>
> (Nemirovich-Danchenko 1968: 46)

It may not immediately be clear what he means by 'everyday features', but Nemirovich's commitment to *simplicity* on stage and his call for a vivid *expressivity* in the performer are characteristics clearly reflected in the later practice of Meyerhold. Even more important, perhaps, is the implicit relationship indicated here between the inner and outer work of the performer – *psychological movements* as Nemirovich calls them – for this all-important relationship, often referred to as *psycho-physicality*, is a dominant theme in the Russian tradition of acting and we will encounter it in many guises in this book.

MEYERHOLD, STANISLAVSKY AND *THE SEAGULL*

Meyerhold (see Figure 1.1) graduated from the Moscow Philharmonic in March 1898, sharing the top prize for acting with Olga Knipper – Chekhov's future wife and soon-to-be star of the MAT. Nemirovich had already seen the potential of the young artist, describing him in his memoirs as having 'excellent directing quality and not a little technical skill' (Nemirovich-Danchenko 1968: 123).

Both graduates joined the newly founded Art Theatre that year, as the talent drawn from both Stanislavsky's Circle and Nemirovich's school was merged to form the revolutionary new theatre. But although he had begun as an advocate of Meyerhold's, Nemirovich's support of him did not last and he offered no resistance when the company was reorganised in 1902, leaving the young actor without a job.

In the intervening four years (1898–1902), Meyerhold played an impressive range of parts (eighteen roles, from blind prophets to princes), developed a passion for Chekhov's writing and, most significantly, observed a highly innovative and self-critical actor-director at work. Of all Meyerhold's creative relationships, his time with Stanislavsky was the most influential, not because Meyerhold followed in his teacher's footsteps – he didn't – but because the two men shared a fundamental belief in the complete training of an actor and in the need to experiment continually. Stanislavsky's famous System did not begin to be formulated until 1906, after Meyerhold had left the MAT, but his first experiments in realising a text with the emphasis on psychological truth were already being made as early as 1898 – with the revival of Chekhov's text, *The Seagull*.

After taking the role of Vassily Shouisky in the inaugural production of the Art Theatre, *Tsar Fyodor Ivanovitch* in October 1898, Meyerhold was given the pivotal role of Konstantin Treplev in Stanislavsky's production of *The Seagull*. Kostia (Treplev's diminutive name) is a young experimental playwright, still living in the shadow of his successful actress mother, Arkadina, and fighting to assert his independence as a writer. He is deeply in love with Nina, another aspiring young artist, and casts her in his own highly stylised and symbolic play-within-a-play. Sitting in the audience at Treplev's play is the already established writer, Trigorin, Arkadina's lover. Trigorin, though, soon develops an amorous interest in Nina, becoming Kostia's rival in both professional and personal terms. Thus, the fortunes of the young

Figure 1.1 Portrait of the young Meyerhold, 1898

moderniser, Kostia, are contrasted with the older Trigorin (representing a kind of established orthodoxy), with Nina as focal point.

This typically Chekhovian love triangle was given a further twist by the casting of Stanislavsky as Trigorin. Critics have been quick to point out the uncanny similarities between the power dynamic at work in the MAT and that reflected in Chekhov's play, especially when you imagine these words being spoken by the young innovator, Meyerhold/Treplev:

> What we need are new artistic forms. And if we don't get new forms it would be better if we had nothing at all.

> (Chekhov 1991: 63)

It wasn't long before Meyerhold himself was saying as much, criticising the Naturalism of the MAT and forging the same theatrical path as Treplev: towards Symbolism and a theatre of stasis. As Nina remarks of Treplev's play: 'It doesn't have much action, your play – it's just a kind of recitation' (Chekhov 1991: 66).

A BAPTISM OF FIRE: THE FELLOWSHIP OF THE NEW DRAMA

Between being sacked by the MAT Board in 1902 and his return to Moscow in 1905, Meyerhold was busy. He seems to have put contingency plans in place for his inevitable ousting from the MAT, booking a theatre south of Moscow in the Ukraine for the next season, 1902–3. Here, in Kherson, Meyerhold joined up with another forced exile – Aleksandr Kosheverov – and, with a troupe of disaffected actors from the MAT, founded what was eventually called The Fellowship of the New Drama. Meyerhold's industry during this season and the next (1903–4) is captured explicitly in the appendix of Meyerhold premières in Robert Leach's book, *Vsevolod Meyerhold* (1989: 194–6): three pages of productions, 140 in all, with Meyerhold taking forty-four roles himself, as well as finding time to translate Georg Hauptmann's text, *Before Sunrise*, from the original German.

What greater baptism of fire can one imagine? Before The Fellowship, Meyerhold had had precious little directing experience. Relatively speaking, he had lots of time to work on his roles and to reflect on the nature of his task as an actor at the MAT. With his days in Kherson often involving the launch of two new productions in a single day, Meyerhold had little time to innovate – or to engage in the pre-rehearsal discussions he argued had been lacking in Stanislavsky's approach. But he did necessarily grapple with the practical difficulties of staging Russian classics (Gogol, Ostrovsky), European Naturalism (Ibsen, Hauptmann, Zola), his beloved Chekhov (*The Seagull*, *The Wedding*, *The Cherry Orchard*) and Shakespeare (*A Midsummer Night's Dream*, *The Merchant of Venice*). He also began his relationship with Maeterlinck, unconsciously laying the foundations for a return to Moscow in decidedly different circumstances from those in which he left.

By 1905 the MAT was seven years old and its founders, Nemirovich and Stanislavsky, were recognising the need to introduce new blood and to reflect more clearly the contemporary movements in Western drama. Stanislavsky's own words, penned in his autobiography, *My Life in Art* (1924), are interestingly more redolent of Treplev's than Trigorin's:

> Like me, [Meyerhold] sought for something new in art, for something more contemporary and modern in spirit. The difference between us lay in the fact that I only strained toward the new, without knowing any of the ways for reaching and realizing it, while Meierhold thought that he had already found new ways and methods which he could not realize partly because of material conditions, and partly due to the weak personnel of the troupe . . . I decided to help Meierhold in his new labors, which as it seemed to me then, agreed with many of my dreams at the time.
>
> (Stanislavsky 1980: 429–30)

Stanislavsky's assessment, written some nineteen years after the events he is describing, was accurate on a number of counts: Meyerhold *did* represent a modernist challenge to the orthodox repertoire of the MAT and he was, in all aspects of his life, responsive to the 'contemporary . . . spirit' or Zeitgeist. It was for this reason that he later embraced the scientific theories of the reflexologist, Pavlov, and why he brought in the constructivist artists Popova and Stepanova to work with him just after the Revolution.

THE THEATRE STUDIO AND *THE DEATH OF TINTAGILES*

Meyerhold's love of innovation may also explain why he accepted Stanislavsky's invitation to return to his Alma Mater as co-director of the Theatre Studio. For this project, entirely funded by Stanislavsky's own money and therefore independent of the main theatre, offered Meyerhold an opportunity to develop an alternative directorial approach – what he called *stylisation*. He had recognised the challenges posed by symbolist texts during his time with the Fellowship and had offered a sensitive reading of Chekhov's symbolic last play *The Cherry Orchard*. But with three productions a week to put on in Kherson, he plainly did not have enough time to devote to any kind of training for his actors, least of all a training in the kind of stylised, highly gestural acting he was looking for in his vision of Maeterlinck's plays.

The Theatre Studio offered him that space. It was, in Stanislavsky's words, 'a *laboratory* for more or less mature actors' (1980: 430, my italics). As such, it embodied the principles of innovation, stylistic experimentation and secluded interrogation which Meyerhold sought to reproduce in many different contexts later in life.

In cultural terms, the move from Naturalism (the attempt to *recreate* life on stage in all its detail) to Symbolism (the attempt to *evoke* and *suggest* a life beyond the material world) was not entirely surprising. Over a decade earlier, the French theatre had fought the same battle – with André Antoine's tiny Théâtre Libre, the bastion of fourth-wall Naturalism, giving way to the symbolist stages of the Théâtre d'Art and Lugné Poe's Théâtre de l'Œuvre. In a sense, the Russian theatre was simply staging the same theatrical revolution as France had done ten years earlier.

But in acknowledging that they needed a counter-repertoire of non-naturalistic plays, Stanislavsky and Nemirovich were echoing a tension felt by the naturalists themselves. Many of the key movers in Naturalism – Ibsen, Strindberg, Hauptmann and (in a different way) Chekhov – all seem to have found the restrictions of Naturalism too great and, as a consequence, allowed their ideas to move into other fields of drama. Strindberg's *Miss Julie* may have had a preface hailing the birth of Naturalism, but his emphasis on the symbolism of the props (the beheaded greenfinch as a symbol of Julie's impending fate, for example) and the atmospheric lighting in the play already signed a progression away from the material conditions of the kitchen sink towards a more implicit realm of communication.

It was this implicit realm, a suggestive, obscure and imaginative world, which Meyerhold tried to create in his Theatre Studio and, specifically, in his production of Maeterlinck's *The Death of Tintagiles*. Here, Meyerhold looked back to his own fascination with music and with theatrical simplicity to define an approach which exploited both characteristics. Movement was kept to a minimum, with Meyerhold defining what gestures the actors could make in a prescriptive 'score' or prompt copy. All the energy of the actor was concentrated into the eyes and lips, creating what Meyerhold called an 'exterior calm which covers volcanic emotions' (Braun 1991: 54). Maeterlinck's words were not spoken naturalistically but 'coldly coined . . . free from the familiar break in the voice' (ibid.) and the effect must have been rather like a sleepwalker concealing a terrible story. All of this was performed in front of a single backdrop – at first just plain – and underscored by a musical accompaniment which was designed to complement exactly the stylised action.

Resisting the usual three-dimensional models, the designers for this production (Nikolai Sapunov and Sergei Sudeikin) painted impressionistic pictures to capture the atmosphere of the plays. The intention was to keep the stage as dark as possible, so as to let the audience complete the story in their own minds and thus, as Meyerhold put it, be transformed into a 'vigilant observer' (Braun 1991: 56). The essence of Meyerhold's symbolist approach is therefore made clear: to enhance the imaginative input of the spectator by *making strange* the actor's body and voice and placing them in a darkened, non-specific theatrical environment. *Plasticity* (the movements of the actor) works alongside *musicality* (in the voices of the actors and in the composer's score) to create a sometimes harmonious, sometimes dissonant theatrical effect.

For Stanislavsky, viewing the dress rehearsal of *The Death of Tintagiles* in October 1905, this strangeness added nothing to its credibility. He had seen an earlier rehearsal in a small workshop space during the summer of that year and had been impressed. But now in the larger proposed home of the Theatre Studio, with no fewer than 700 seats (Braun 1995: 41), the intended suggestive style was lost. This was exacerbated by Stanislavsky's insistence that the lights should be turned up, killing the symbolist aura of other-worldliness and revealing the holes in Meyerhold's production.

By the end of that year Meyerhold had left the MAT for a second time and was bound for St Petersburg. But he did not leave Moscow empty-handed. For he had experienced a model of discipline, of innovation and of expressive acting in his time with Stanislavsky which was to have a lasting impression on his work, a debt he was happy to acknowledge:

> You who knew Stanislavsky only in his old age can't possibly imagine what a powerful actor he was. If I have become somebody, it is only because of the years I spent alongside him. Mark this well.
>
> (Gladkov 1997: 149)

In St Petersburg, Meyerhold rekindled his interest in Maeterlinck and by the next year was directing one of the most celebrated names of the Russian theatre, Vera Komissarzhevskaya, at her own Dramatichesky Theatre in another of his plays, *Sister Beatrice*. Thus began an extended period (from 1906–17) living and working in what was then the capital of Russia.

ST PETERSBURG (1906–17)

VERA KOMISSARZHEVSKAYA

From a distance it is hard to see why Meyerhold and Komissarzhevskaya (1864–1910) formed a working relationship: he, a relatively inexperienced graduate of an art theatre, dedicated to the pursuit of new forms and she, a widely known actress of the State theatre, famed for her naturalistic roles playing Ibsen's Nora and Nina in the first ever production of Chekhov's play in 1896.

The daughter of one of Stanislavsky's early collaborators, Fedor Komissarzhevsky, Vera Fedorovna Komissarzhevskaya began working in the theatre in 1892 and from 1896 to 1902 rose to stardom as the principal actress at the State-supported Imperial Theatre – the Aleksandrinsky – in St Petersburg. She was, in many ways, one of the first method actors. She had a reputation for accepting roles close to her own nature and for engaging emotionally with the character at a very deep level. 'My nature requires me to feel with my characters,' she argued: 'I don't know how to act any other way. I have to wash each role in the blood of my own heart' (Schuler 1996: 166).

Such emotionalism would not have recommended her to Meyerhold. His own acting style was reserved and he harboured a deep-seated distrust of unrestrained passions in performance. This was, in part, due to a disturbing experience in his early life in which he empathised so closely with the title role of a play called *The Madman* that he began to consider himself deranged: 'I lived every line,' his biographer, Nikolai Volkov, records him saying, 'I thought I was insane' (Hoover 1974: 5).

Much of Meyerhold's later work reflects the fear he had of this kind of hypnotic acting and his repudiation of Naturalism is often seen in the same light, as a rejection of psychologically driven drama. Why, then, did he collaborate with Komissarzhevskaya, an actress who excelled on both counts?

One answer is that they shared the same desire to refresh the repertoire of the Russian theatre. Another, more cynical suggestion, comes from Catherine Schuler:

> Meyerhold came to St. Petersburg not because he believed in Komissarzhev-skaia's vision or mission but because a contract with the Dramaticheskii Theatre was a ticket out of the provinces.
>
> (Schuler 1996: 174)

Certainly, Meyerhold had learnt from his days in Kherson (and from a revived attempt to stage a modern repertoire in Tiflis, after the failure of the Theatre Studio) that producing the 'New Drama' in such provincial circumstances was never going to be easy. St Petersburg, he must have thought, offered him a far more discerning audience as well as a flourishing avant-garde movement.

But although the latter was true (Meyerhold did mix with range of artistic modernisers including many symbolists in St Petersburg), this did not save him from accusations of betrayal and of pretentious-ness, specifically for his treatment of Ibsen in his première production. His new directorial approach was first seen with *Hedda Gabler*, a naturalistic text, written by Ibsen in 1890 and dealing with some of the Norwegian's favourite themes: inheritance, power, social influence. Meyerhold's production, though, was anything but naturalistic. With Komissarzhevskaya in the title role, Meyerhold wanted to challenge directly the style for which she was renowned and which had come to characterise his old hunting ground, the MAT:

> Is life really like this? Is this what Ibsen wrote? Life is not like this, and it is not what Ibsen wrote. *Hedda Gabler* on the stage of the dramatic theatre is *stylised*. Its aim is to reveal Ibsen's play to the spectator by employing new unfamiliar means of scenic presentation.
>
> (Braun 1991: 66)

These new means of expression included a timeless costume design which aimed to capture the *essence* of the character. Oversized furniture was used to break up the natural perspective for the audience and the stage space itself was distorted, flattened, to provide a playing area just twelve feet deep. Spectators were not simply peeping in on a room full of people living their lives, as the Naturalism of the play demands, but viewing a scene in which the space itself suggested the thematic concerns of the play – a 'cold majesty', as Meyerhold puts it (Braun 1991: 67).

Meyerhold's work on *Sister Beatrice* (see Figure 1.2) continued this stylised approach, although here the text lent itself more readily to such treatment. Once again, Komissarzhevskaya took the title role and once again the depth of the stage was limited. In this instance Meyerhold had his cast working on a platform just seven feet deep – no deeper than the average bathroom – although the width of the stage was far greater. The result was a kind of theatre sculpture – or bas-relief – in which Komissarzhevskaya and company were grouped into starkly expressive tableaux, reminiscent of religious paintings. Following the work he had done at the Studio on *The Death of Tintagiles*, the gestural language of the actors was carefully prescribed and choreographed so that together the ensemble created a predominantly pictorial impression. Meyerhold actually brought paintings into the rehearsal room as a stimulus, merging the different shapes to create a new but nevertheless highly orchestrated look to the production.

With all these anti-illusionary devices in place, Komissarzhevskaya's specifically empathetic style of acting had to adapt in some way, although, interestingly, she did not reject all of her previous techniques. She still personalised the role and still drew on her inner resources to lend an energetic charge to it. At the same time, her voice captured the stylised musicality Meyerhold had been looking for in his first Maeterlinck production at the Theatre Studio. Frantisek Deák has documented the production in some detail:

Figure 1.2 *Sister Beatrice*, 1906

> Komissarzhevskaya used two different voices. The voice for the Virgin Mary
> was like 'pure sound of an unknown musical instrument', a depersonalized
> sound. The voice for Beatrice, even when keeping with the rhythm imposed by
> Meyerhold, had certain emotional undertones and personal quality . . . It is
> quite possible that Komissarzhevskaya's identification with the part, which was
> against the Symbolist esthetic of a detached representation, was one of the
> reasons for the great success of the production.

(Deák 1982: 50)

Unfortunately, *Sister Beatrice* was alone in being both critically and commercially acclaimed. Other productions failed, due either to the cast's unease with Meyerhold's experimentation or to the inappropriateness of the lead role for an ageing principal actress. Meyerhold's relationship with Komissarzhevskaya began to show its weaknesses and his time at her theatre was running out. But there was one more major event to grace the stage of the Dramatichesky Theatre, an event which fitted perfectly Meyerhold's ideal of a divided audience: his production of the symbolist farce, *The Fairground Booth* (1906).

MEYERHOLD, BLOK AND THE *BALAGAN*

By the time Meyerhold produced his play in December 1906, Aleksandr Blok (1880–1921) had already made his name as a poet and was an established figure in St Petersburg literary circles. His early work was charged with a darkly romantic spirit and was often inspired by his relationships – actual or virtual – with women. As an adolescent he had fallen for a married woman twice his age and captured this youthful spark of love in his writing:

> I did not know, unhappy one, that embraces were so hot. . . . She, inflamed with
> the fire of passion, wanted to melt my heart. . . . She boiled with love's desire!
> But I held my mind captive with a cold thought, and only at moments, ardently,
> I believed and thirsted.

(Forsyth 1977: 20–1)

Even in the flush of adolescent hormones one can detect a sense of detachment in this extract, an ability of Blok's to sit back from the experience and apply a 'cold thought' to the proceedings. Such critical detachment is evident in far greater measure in his first play, *The Fairground Booth*, or, in Russian, *Balaganchik*.

In addition to a booth at fairs, *Balagan* also has associated meanings – farce, clown, playacting, showman – all of which mark a distinct shift in tone from the sombre statuesque atmosphere of *Sister Beatrice*. In fact, Blok's drama openly ridicules the portentous seriousness of the symbolist movement, revelling instead in the characteristics of the popular theatre: audience involvement, riotous action, unashamed theatricality.

In part, this shift in allegiance – for Blok was considered to be 'the greatest Symbolist' (Banham 1992: 103) – was stimulated by a growing sense of pessimism and a desire by Blok to satirise his own troublesome relationships in dramatic form. The narrative thread to the play thus bears a marked similarity to the complicated love triangle he himself was immersed in at the time. His wife, Lyubov Mendelyeva (Columbine in the play) had fallen in love with another famous symbolist writer, Andrei Bely (Harlequin), with Blok (Pierrot) the lamenting victim:

> PIERROT.　Where are you faithless one? . . .
> 　　　　　Beneath your window, plaintively,
> 　　　　　My guitar will twang as you whirl with friends.
> 　　　　　I'll rouge my face that glimmers moonily,
> 　　　　　Pencil eyebrows, stick a moustache on.
> 　　　　　My poor heart – can you hear it, Columbine
> 　　　　　Sobbing out its melancholy song?
>
> 　　　　　　　　　　　　　　　　　　(Green 1986: 48)

Perhaps we should note here that, in real life, Blok was far from an innocent victim and engaged in the same infidelities as his wife. In his drama, though, the love triangle drives the simple plot, with Harlequin/ Bely leading Columbine/Mendelyeva away to enjoy a wintry sleigh ride and Pierrot/Blok following dejectedly after.

It is here, at the moment in the play most steeped in romantic imagery – soft snow falling, sleigh bells chiming – that Blok's sense of detachment (his 'cold thought') surfaces, not to dampen the atmosphere but to inject a mischievous vein of humour:

> PIERROT.　O in his toils he'd entangled her,
> 　　　　　With laughter and jingling bells.
> 　　　　　Then he drew her wrap about her
> 　　　　　And flat on her face she fell!
>
> 　　　　　　　　　　　　　　　　　　(Green 1986: 52)

In fact, Columbine has turned into a cardboard cut-out and Pierrot and Harlequin spend the rest of the evening walking the streets together, gazing not into the eyes of their mutual love but nestling cheek to cheek with each other!

Blok never takes himself too seriously in this play. Nor does he allow his characters to get caught up in predictable theatrical situations. Instead, they exhibit a refreshing sense of self-irony and are capable of making huge emotional shifts: from jealous desperation to glee, from ardent passion to whimsical disinterest. For all these reasons Blok's *Fairground Booth* was a model of the kind of drama Meyerhold wanted to produce.

From the Symbolism of Maeterlinck Meyerhold had found a distinct *physical* approach to performance, an expressive mode of non-naturalistic acting which characterised much of his later work. But the symbolists were often accused of being removed from reality in their mystical pursuit of the immaterial, an accusation which Meyerhold could not bear. Blok satirises this characteristic in his play, opening the drama with a chorus of Mystics who exude all the signs of Symbolism to a deliberately laughable degree. At the same time Blok is drawing on a number of conventions associated with a much older tradition of theatre, a tradition to which Meyerhold became inextricably connected and which he wrote about at length later in his career: the popular theatre.

It will already be evident in the extracts from *The Fairground Booth* that the dramatis personae (Blok's list of characters) bears no resemblance either to Naturalism or to Symbolism. Blok is not trying to represent real people with real names. Nor is he attempting to revive the dark atmosphere of castles and knights. Instead, he is looking to the popular tradition of *commedia dell'arte* for his characters, a theatrical form which first grew up in Europe in the sixteenth and seventeenth centuries and which in part informs the English pantomime. Let us spend a minute detailing the key characteristics of this all-important form of theatre.

COMMEDIA DELL'ARTE

Commedia dell'arte was founded on stock characters including Harlequin (or Arlecchino), Pierrot and Columbine, Blok's three chosen types, as well as a host of others such as Pantalone and Il Dottore (the doctor). It was an improvised form, based loosely around scenarios and punctuated with moments of comic business or *lazzi*. Before it became drawn into the establishment (it was eventually scripted and lost its spark), *commedia* was performed in a wide range of public places, adapting to every space with its flexible, booth-like staging. It was predominantly concerned with matters of sex and status, pitting servants against masters in endless comic mishaps. Primarily an external form of theatre, the *commedia* actors were not burdened with creating psychologically coherent characters, but were free to improvise using a conventional physical language instantly recognisable to the audience. Most of the characters wore a half-mask, revealing the mouth and chin but concealing the more expressive part of the face. These masks were often distorted with large noses and prominent features, giving rise to an exaggerated sense of character. *Commedia* was 'popular' because it did not rely heavily on the written word. It was a visual form, brought *to* the people by a travelling troupe of professionals and pitched at a local level. As a mask-based performance it was played outwards, making a direct connection with its spectators and engaging them in a two-way relationship.

For Meyerhold, who himself played Pierrot in Blok's play, the spirit of *commedia* was significant in many ways. First, because it placed more emphasis on the *physical* craft of the actor. *Commedia* performance was a highly skilled job and called on many aspects of an actor's training, aspects which Meyerhold believed had been undervalued in the Russian theatre of the early 1900s: physical dexterity, precision, balance, heightened expressiveness. Second, it established a different relationship between the actor and the text, empowering the performer to grab the audience's attention through their own improvisatory skill. Third, the *commedia* characters were types – masks – and were not therefore bound by the psychological laws Stanislavsky was attempting to uncover in his System. People were not asked to *believe* in them in the same way as they were to believe in Treplev or Nora. Instead, the masks could be seen for what they were, fictional dramatic creations fulfilling a function within the overall piece. Finally, *commedia* captured the spirit of surprise which we have already seen Blok exploiting in *The Fairground Booth*. Rather than the slow build-up of tension – the incrementally structured rhythms of Naturalism – *commedia*, and by extension Meyerhold's theatre, could undergo sharp changes in atmosphere and collisions of ideas and of styles, all of which were designed to keep the audience alert and responsive.

Writing six years after the production of Blok's play, Meyerhold was drawn back to the *commedia* characters of *The Fairground Booth* to illustrate this particular characteristic (what we will later come to understand as the *grotesque*):

> Depth and extract, brevity and contrast! No sooner has the pale, lanky Pierrot crept across the stage, no sooner has the spectator sensed in his movements the eternal tragedy of mutely suffering mankind, than the apparition is succeeded by the merry Harlequinade. The tragic gives way to the comic, harsh satire replaces the sentimental ballad.
>
> (Braun 1991: 137)

MEYERHOLD'S *FAIRGROUND BOOTH*

In Meyerhold's production of *Balaganchik* these surprising shifts of tone, already endemic to Blok's style, were intensified by his directorial choices. The chorus of Mystics, who in Blok's original disappear into their own costumes like burst effigies, in Meyerhold's production transform into cardboard statues, mirroring the demise of Columbine and setting up the absurd entrance of the Author perfectly:

> Ladies and Gentlemen! I apologize to you most humbly, but I must disclaim all responsibility! They are making a laughing stock of me! I wrote a perfectly realistic play.
>
> (Green 1986: 51)

Accentuating the already obvious theatricality of the piece, Meyerhold placed the whole of the action in a booth of its own:

> This booth has its own stage, curtain, prompter's box and proscenium opening. Instead of being masked by the conventional border, the flies, together with all the ropes and wires, are visible to the audience; when the entire set is hauled aloft in the booth, the audience in the actual theatre sees the whole process.
>
> (Braun 1991: 70)

The best way to gauge whether such starkly self-conscious theatricality (what we now call *meta-theatricality*) was effective is to examine the audience's reaction. Meyerhold intended his spectators to be anything but passive and, on the first night on 30 December 1906, they reacted in just the way he wanted. It was proof of what he called 'true theatricality':

> The auditorium was in uproar as though it were a real battle. Solid, respectable citizens were ready to come to blows; whistles and roars of anger alternated with piercing howls conveying a mixture of fervour, defiance, anger and despair: 'Blok – Sapunov [the designer] – Kuzmin [the composer] – M-e-y-e-r-h-o-l-d, B-r-a-v-o-o-o.'
>
> (Braun 1995: 65–6)

What better response could the director dedicated to splitting his audience's allegiances and to fomenting controversy have wished for? It was testament to Meyerhold's directorial vision and to the modernism of Blok's text that there was such an emphatic reaction to the production – a production which we can now say was one the most significant of all of Meyerhold's experiments.

Meyerhold remained in post as artistic director at Komissarzhevskaya's theatre for almost another year, but, after repeated differences of opinion with the rest of the management, parted company with the theatre in November 1907.

For Komissarzhevskaya, the collaboration had been little short of a disaster. She had received very few good notices and had placed the theatre's finances in a precarious position. For Meyerhold, the results of his time with Vera Fedorovna could be measured in very different terms. Via Blok, he had begun a lifelong association with *commedia* and with the popular theatre in general. He had concluded a brief but highly influential period of experimentation with symbolist theatre, devising an aesthetic of stylisation and of musicality which informed much of his later work. And, perhaps most significantly, he had started to dismantle the conventions of the theatre at their very base, producing a style of heightened theatricality and of shocking unpredictability which shaped both his training methods and his work as a director.

SERVANT OF THE STATE OR UNDERGROUND SUBVERSIVE? THE IMPERIAL THEATRES AND THE DEVELOPMENT OF THE STUDIOS

The years at Komissarzhevskaya's theatre had cast Meyerhold in the role of a radical reformer – a reputation which carried far and wide.

The path, seemingly, was set out for him: to develop the laboratory work he had begun in Moscow with Stanislavsky and continued in St Petersburg and to consolidate his search for 'new forms' as a director. The best place to do such work must surely have been in the studios and intimate theatres in which he had begun this quest. But Meyerhold did not continue in this direction, at least not visibly. Instead, he took his chance in the theatres which seemed most in opposition to his project of reform – the Imperial Theatres. It was a typically unpredictable move, taking Meyerhold into the world of large-scale, State-funded performance. The Imperial Theatres, numbering five in all, were based in St Petersburg and Moscow and in many ways were the antithesis of the art theatre movement in which Meyerhold had flourished: there was a deeply ingrained hierarchy among the actors and no tradition of the director being a creative artist, as Meyerhold saw the role.

Meyerhold was appointed director to the St Petersburg Imperial Theatres in April 1908 by the chief administrator Vladimir Telyakovsky, a man who clearly shared the young director's contrary attitude to life:

> I became interested in him when I heard unflattering opinions of him on all sides. When everyone attacks a man, he must be of some importance.
>
> (Hoover 1974: 51)

Thus began almost a decade of work for Meyerhold, taking him from the aftermath of one failed revolution (in 1905) to the very day in which the Tsarist regime began finally to crumble for good, in February 1917.

The pace of production slowed considerably in his new job. No longer was Meyerhold overseeing the kind of hectic schedule he had experienced in the provinces. Here, he could enjoy a lengthy period of research similar to that which Stanislavsky and Nemirovich had called for back in 1898, although in a very different environment to the MAT. He read avidly, wrote articles and collaborated closely with artists and choreographers, including the designer Aleksandr Golovin.

But with only two productions a season to direct, Meyerhold did not simply spend his time preparing for the operas and classics he was to direct at the Imperial Theatres. Instead, he 'moonlighted' as director and teacher on a range of small-scale, innovative ventures, in conditions which could not be more different from the Aleksandrinsky or

Marinsky Theatres: cabaret venues, tiny stages, rooms in his own flat and in others' houses. Meyerhold, in effect, began to live two very different lives – the one public and high profile, the other low key and exclusive. It was a theatrical twist to his own existence which Meyerhold must have relished.

DR DAPERTUTTO

Meyerhold's double life was given further dramatic symbolism when he adopted the pseudonym, Dr Dapertutto (see Figure 1.3), a character created by one of his favourite authors, E.T.A. Hoffmann, and who symbolised many of the contradictory qualities Meyerhold saw in himself. Taking on the role of Dapertutto allowed Meyerhold to continue his experimental work without breaking his contract with the Imperial Theatres. It was a compromise from the management which had far-reaching implications, for without the 'other side' to his work Meyerhold would not have begun his programme of teaching or have developed his interest in the popular theatre. Both of these strands, as we shall see, had much to do with his theatrical direction after the Revolution.

In an article entitled 'The Fairground Booth', written in the middle of his Dapertutto period, in 1912, Meyerhold defined his aspirations for the future by recalling the past:

> The cult of the cabotinage, which I am sure will reappear with the restoration of the theatre of the past, will help the modern actor to rediscover the basic laws of theatricality.

(Braun 1991: 126)

The cabotin was a strolling player, able, as Meyerhold puts it, 'to work miracles with his technical mastery' and capable of keeping 'alive the tradition of the true art of acting' (Braun 1991: 122). He was a model of the kind of self-aware, physically dynamic style of performance we have already seen in Blok's play of the same name. But Meyerhold was not just celebrating old alliances in this article. He was defining his own way of working for decades to come: a fusion of traditional and modern theatrical techniques. Tradition was assured by Meyerhold's continued interest in popular forms, including *commedia dell'arte*. The 'new' was to be found in his collaborations with contemporary playwrights,

Figure 1.3 Grigoriev's portrait of Dr Dapertutto, 1916

designers and composers as well as in the terminology which began to emerge later from the experimental work. Meyerhold's message was simple: in order to innovate you have to renovate – and he meant the popular theatres of old.

His production of *Columbine's Scarf*, freely adapted from a pantomime by Arthur Schnitzler and staged as part of a varied programme of events in a tiny theatre in October 1910, illustrates this idea. Returning to the story of Pierrot, Harlequin and Columbine, Meyerhold worked closely with the designer Nikolai Sapunov to create what Konstantin Rudnitsky calls 'chaotic and dynamic stage designs' (Rudnitsky 1988: 15). The physicality and magical trickery with props in this production owed a significant debt to the *commedia* style but the *grotesque* imagery and atmosphere achieved by Meyerhold and Sapunov spoke directly to the contemporary concerns of the country. As Meyerhold's biographer, Volkov states: they 'saw clearly into the ugliness of everyday life in Russia' (Braun 1995: 101). Such a mixture of old and new pre-empts the approach Meyerhold took in 1926 with his masterpiece production of Gogol's *The Government Inspector* and we will be looking in detail at this work in Chapter 3. But it also characterises a general tendency of Meyerhold's work to synthesise the ancient and modern, an approach begun at the Dramatichesky Theatre with Komissarzhevskaya and developed in the guise of Dapertutto.

MEYERHOLD'S STUDIOS

Meyerhold's teaching programme, designed to create this 'modern actor', was also formulated under the name of Dapertutto and looked again to *commedia* for inspiration. Having taught acting technique in a music, drama and opera school in 1909, Meyerhold formed a specialised group two years later, along with the young director, Vladimir Solovyov, to continue his research into *commedia* techniques. Principal among their repertoire was the one-act play *Harlequin the Marriage Broker*, penned by Solovyov himself in the manner of a *commedia* scenario. Meyerhold's own description of the harlequinade captures the knockabout style very effectively:

> Striking one's rival across the face . . . one character carrying off another pick-a-back; fights, blows with clubs, cutting off of noses with wooden swords.
>
> (Braun 1991: 145)

Here, in this improvised theatre piece, are the seeds of what was later to be called biomechanics – Meyerhold's acting system, devised as a counterpoint to Stanislavsky's System (with a capital 'S'). After the Revolution, these loosely defined *lazzi* became tightly controlled études such as 'The Slap', 'The Stab with the Dagger' and 'Throwing the Stone', names which betray their history in Italian popular theatre and which, as we shall see in Chapter 4, are still taught by Russian masters today.

At this stage, though, the work had not been fully formalised. Instead, it was music which provided the controlling influence among the playfulness:

> The actor . . . is free to act *ex improvisio*. However the actor's freedom is only relative because he is subject to the discipline of the musical score.
>
> (Braun 1991: 144)

We may recall that Meyerhold's early work with Maeterlinck placed great stress on the musical score. Indeed, almost all of the significant production work of Meyerhold relied heavily on the musical accompaniment devised by the composer as well as on the essential *musicality* of the performers. Here, Meyerhold is making clear that the discipline of music (in tension with the freedom of improvisation) is as fundamental to an actor's training programme as it is to the production work – two sides of the theatrical equation which Meyerhold was to bring together after the Revolution.

By 1914 Meyerhold was including Shakespeare and Spanish theatre in his teaching, as well as examples of the modern drama in Russia. A year earlier (in September 1913) he had secured a specified venue for an actor's Studio and now he was beginning to clarify its aims. These included a detailed study of *commedia* techniques, run by Solovyov, exercises in rhythm, and movement classes devised by Meyerhold himself. In the same year (1914) his Studio published the first of nine editions of a journal entitled *The Love of Three Oranges*, in which the practical activities of the Studio were documented and dramatic scenarios, poems and critical articles were published. Aleksandr Blok remained a collaborator on this project, heading up the poetry section, but Meyerhold took overall editorial control.

A 1916 edition of the periodical illustrates just how far the aims of the training had extended. Among thirteen subjects highlighted for discussion, the following areas of expertise are listed:

- the comic, tragic and tragicomic (or grotesque) masks;
- the nineteenth century Russian classics including Gogol;
- the popular theatre, the circus, and the Hindu and Oriental theatres;
- contemporary theories of the theatre, including Meyerhold's own;
- the role of the director and designer.

(Braun 1991: 153–4)

It was a daunting and highly ambitious list, illustrating just how highly Meyerhold valued the past theatrical contributions of both East and West and pointing clearly to the kind of actor he wanted to create: rounded, informed and flexible.

MASQUERADE

Whilst Meyerhold developed this laboratory of actor training, he was continuing in his role as Imperial Theatre director, overseeing highly elaborate, some might say extravagant, theatrical (and operatic) spectacles. The ultimate in this alternative strand of work, the jewel in his double life, was his production of Lermontov's *Masquerade* in 1917 (see Figure 1.4). In all aspects *Masquerade* was a grand production. It had taken seven years to come to fruition, delayed by the onset of war in 1914 and, according to Marjorie Hoover, by the extensive archival research Meyerhold conducted in preparation (Hoover 1974: 67). It involved a cast of 200, two-thirds of whom were choreographed by Meyerhold in one group in the opulent ball scenes which punctuate the action of the play. Its designs (again by Golovin, Meyerhold's close collaborator in this period) were highly elaborate and technically demanding – nothing was recycled from old stock. And its impact, irrespective of the richness of the settings at this sensitive time in Russian history, was huge – it remained in the repertoire of the Aleksandrinsky theatre until the Second World War.

But for all its grandiose indulgence, Meyerhold's production bore the hallmarks of his earlier work in the experimental theatre. Music underpinned all aspects the performance, the text was rearranged into episodes à la Blok's *Fairground Booth* and the manipulation of props on stage owed a significant debt to his Studio's experiments with *commedia* – indeed, some of the younger actors from the Imperial Theatre attended Meyerhold's laboratory.

Figure 1.4
Masquerade at the Aleksandrinsky, 1917

At the same time, *Masquerade* anticipated some of the techniques Meyerhold was to perfect in his post-revolutionary period, chiefly in terms of its staging. Realizing that the dynamic force of the play would be compromised by lengthy set changes, Meyerhold devised a *mise-en-scène* (setting) which leapt from forestage, to mainstage, to a series of intimate 'substages', sectioned off by screens and borders. The director could thus ensure a swift transition between scenes – the early manifestation of what was later called kinetic staging for his production of *The Government Inspector* – while assuring that the proscenium arch did not act as a barrier between audience and performer.

Meyerhold had come a long way from his days on tour in the provinces. He was now, at the age of forty-three, a significant figure in the mainstream theatre world of tsarist Russia, famed for his highly skilled direction of large casts as well as for the development of an innovative system of actor training. As the shots began to ring out at the beginning of the second Revolution, corresponding exactly with the opening of Meyerhold's *Masquerade*, the question remained: would he be as important a figure in the new world order?

MEYERHOLD AND THE REVOLUTION (1917–22)

Of course, looking back, the answer to that question is easy. Meyerhold's career as a director is best known for his *post*-revolutionary productions, among which must be listed: *Mystery Bouffe* (1918 and 1921), *The Magnanimous Cuckold* (1922), *The Death of Tarelkin* (1922), *The Government Inspector* (1926), *Woe to Wit* (1928) and *The Bedbug* (1929). But at the time it was hardly a foregone conclusion that the Imperial Theatre director would succeed in the transformed political landscape which emerged after February and October 1917.

There are two dates because there were two significant stages to the overthrowing of the Tsar's ruling class. The first February uprising led to what was called the Provisional Government – a compromise in which the Tsar stood down and control of the country was given over to an unelected group of academics, industrialists and lawyers. The Bolsheviks (or Reds) did not recognise the new government and began to return to Russia from exile, sensing that the time had come for a full-scale overturning of the country's power base. Very quickly they began to swell their ranks, mainly with workers, soldiers and sailors, and the party membership rose from a handful of people in February to a third of a million by October (Fitzpatrick 1982: 46). With such growing support, and with the Provisional Government struggling with decisions over the war campaign (there was still one year left of the First World War, remember), the possibilities of a coup – a violent insurrection to overthrow the government – grew. And on 24 October this was what happened: the sitting government, headed by Aleksandr Kerensky, was 'stormed' and subsequently thrown out.

You may be familiar with the famous images created by one of Meyerhold's students, Sergei Eisenstein, which recount this momentous occasion: hordes of soldiers stream into the Winter Palace in St Petersburg (then Petrograd), firing on the resistant enemy and heroically taking the territory of the Palace and with it the power of the country. But these images in Eisenstein's film, *October* (1928), are fictional and romanticised. In reality, there was little or no bloodshed, the battleship Aurora did not fire a shot and Kerensky was let out of a side door and allowed to flee. Even so, there had been a successful overthrowing of the vestiges of the old order and in its stead was Bolshevism.

Meyerhold, who was always responsive to the spirit of the time, reacted quickly to the new powers and within three weeks of the October Revolution had already attended a meeting called by the minister for education and the arts, Anatoly Lunacharsky. He found himself with only four other enthusiasts at this gathering (out of a possible 120) and must have thought that his chosen profession was anything but committed to the new regime. Of the other four who did turn up, he knew Blok and had already met Mayakovsky, the playwright and poet, who was to become one of the most important figures in Meyerhold's career. Very soon Meyerhold was brought on to the board of the new theatre department within Lunacharsky's ministry, The Theatre Department of the Commissariat of Enlightenment (TEO), and by September of the next year (1918) was heading up the Petrograd branch of this organisation. He had also joined the Bolshevik party (see Figure 1.5) and was consciously manoeuvring within the party's bureaucratic structures.

Meyerhold produced Mayakovsky's play *Mystery Bouffe* (the first Soviet play, as it was known) in the same year, for the first anniversary of the Revolution and he went on to direct two others: *The Bedbug* and *The Bathhouse* (1930). *Mystery Bouffe*, in Mayakovsky's own words, is: 'A Heroic, Epic, Satiric Representation of our Era' and this description amply captures the scope and immediacy of his text. It is a modern day

Figure 1.5 Meyerhold the Bolshevik, 1922

parable play, telling the story of the Revolution through a series of biblical episodes which have clear associations with the events of October 1917. Mayakovsky was so keen to see the play reflect the times in which it was being produced that he wrote a small explanatory note to the second version of the play (1921):

> In the future, all persons performing, presenting, reading or publishing *Mystery Bouffe* should change the content, making it contemporary, immediate, up to the minute.
>
> (Mayakovsky 1995: 39)

Meyerhold too wanted to use his immediate cultural and political environment in his work as a director and this may be one reason why he and Mayakovsky collaborated so effectively together. For Meyerhold, the 'change' in response to the Revolution could be seen in the language he began to adopt to express his theatrical thinking. Where before it was the popular theatre which underpinned much of the training system he was devising, now, in the new post-revolutionary climate, it was science and industry, specifically objective psychology and Taylorism. For it was these two areas which the new ruling order wanted to see developed.

BIOMECHANICS, PAVLOV AND TAYLOR

We will analyse in detail the theoretical writings which emerged from this period in Meyerhold's career in the next chapter. But here we can note a distinct change in expression concerning his emergent acting system. After 1917, and specifically after the civil war between the White Army and the Reds had been won, the influences of *commedia*, oriental theatre and the circus were subsumed under the banner of biomechanics, a banner which was waved by Meyerhold and his students in a range of public locations in the early 1920s. This did not mean that he rejected these traditional forms as a basis for his system, but rather that the training system he taught from 1921 in Moscow had a distinctly different method of *articulation* – one which drew on two major figures in the thinking of the time: Ivan Pavlov (the objective psychologist) and Frederick Winslow Taylor (an American industrialist).

Often this scientific basis to Meyerhold's work is criticised for being superficial or badly thought out. Edward Braun calls it 'specious' (Braun

1991: 183), for example – that is a deceptively attractive theory but ultimately a false one. But while Meyerhold served to gain a lot from connecting his work with some of the favoured ideas at the time, he did also find something of practical help in these supposedly unconnected disciplines.

From Pavlov, the man best known for his experiments on dogs, Meyerhold borrowed the idea that behaviour is best understood as a chain of reflex responses to the external world. Pavlov's theory was resolutely objective: we don't act but *react*, in response to the different stimuli of our environment. This pattern of behaviour, Pavlov maintained, was as true for humans as it was for the animals in his laboratory. 'Chain reflexes' (our reactions connected together in a long 'domino line' of responses) are what he calls 'the foundation of the nervous activities of both men and of animals' (Pavlov 1927: 11). Meyerhold tested this idea in his own laboratory, not on dogs but with actors.

From Taylor, Meyerhold took the idea of smoothly executed, rhythmically economical actions. As a man driven to obsession over the question of efficiency, fluent movement was something Taylor himself had been preaching to raise the levels of productivity in factories in America. He broke up the work of his labourers into simple and connected 'tasks' and then gave each task a maximum time in which it could be completed. The aim was high productivity – a watchword of the new Soviet powers too – and Meyerhold pursued it with characteristic vigour. He even called for the 'Taylorization of the theatre' to reduce a four-hour theatre piece to just sixty minutes (Braun 1991: 199).

In theoretical terms, biomechanics is a fusion of these two ideas. It is an objective system, focusing on the external apparatus of the actor and designed to create a responsive, efficient and *productive* actor. Although the work of the performer was far removed from that which was done in the factories, Meyerhold wanted to claim an allegiance with industry. An effective theatre piece (the 'product' of the theatre) is one which 'hits the mark' and succeeds in communicating its message, just as an efficient factory may produce goods without waste and to specification.

CONSTRUCTIVISM IN *THE MAGNANIMOUS CUCKOLD* AND *THE DEATH OF TARELKIN*

Meyerhold was not alone in the pursuit of factory-like efficiency. Concurrent with the developments in industry and science, the fine arts were responding to the shift in emphasis brought about by the Revolution. In no other art movement was this more explicitly captured than in Constructivism. Aleksei Gan, one of the more radical of their number and a kind of Treplev for the modern age, explains:

> The socio-political system conditioned by the new economic structure gives rise to new forms and means of expression. The emergent culture of labor and intellect will be expressed by *intellectual material production*.

> (Bann 1974: 37, my italics)

Although Gan's extremism led him to attack all art, including Meyerhold's, his statement has some affinity with the core of Meyerhold's practice at the time: to focus on conscious, creative *work*. For the constructivists this meant a move away from the art of the easel to sculpture and poster production. For Meyerhold it meant centring attention on the principal material resource of the theatre – the actor's body. For both, the emphasis on *products* led to a celebration of the possibilities of the machine – that which produces things – and this is clearly expressed in the designs Lyubov Popova created for Fernand Crommelynck's *The Magnanimous Cuckold* (see Figures 1.6 and 1.7).

In keeping with the philosophy of the constructivists, Popova transformed the Meyerholdian stage into a machine, casting the actors as workers within the theatre factory. Any attempt at representation was banished beyond the highly stylised wheel which dominated the backdrop (the central character, Bruno, is a miller). Instead of rooms, chairs and realistic properties there were ramps and walkways, and the usual flats, borders and curtains were disposed of to reveal the stark brick wall of the theatre. But while the stage may have resembled the skeletal structure of a huge machine, the actors were not reduced to automatons. They retained all the vigour, playfulness and dexterity of Meyerhold's earlier experiments in *commedia*. As the critic Boris Alpers explains:

> The strong, agile, physically robust actor filled the stage with his self-possessed movements. It was as though he impersonated the new man freed from the power of things.

> (Symons 1971: 84)

Thus, Meyerhold effected yet another fusion of old and new, bringing on to his stage what James M. Symons tellingly calls 'twentieth century,

Figure 1.6
Model
reconstruction
of *The
Magnanimous
Cuckold*, 1922

Figure 1.7
Three actors
in *The
Magnanimous
Cuckold*, 1922

CABOTIN = poser, ham (actor)

machine-age versions of that cabotin of whom Meyerhold had spoken so fondly in 1912' (ibid.: 83). Alma Law has documented the whole production in some detail and the mixture of slapstick, *commedia*-style acting with the modernist environment of Popova's constructivist set comes through very clearly in her descriptions:

> The construction aided the actors in much the same way that a properly designed machine enables a worker to perform more efficiently. . . . The action demanded acrobatic virtuosity and split second timing as a whirlwind of blows, leaps, falls and somersaults all but swallowed up Crommelynck's text.
>
> (1982: 71–2)

In the same year (1922) Meyerhold collaborated with another Constructivist, Varvara Stepanova. For the production of *The Death of Tarelkin*, by Aleksandr Sukhovo-Kobylin, Stepanova produced a similar machine-like set, this time with a huge meat mincer-cum-cage as the centrepiece. She also created stylised costumes, akin to the uniforms worn by convicts, and so retained the anti-illusionary approach of her colleague, Popova. Once again, the moving parts of the set were complemented by the dynamism of the actors and the pictures which survive of the production indicate a style of acting which was close to that seen in American film comedies featuring the Keystone Cops and Charlie Chaplin.

There were other experiments, but these two productions capture the essence of the union of biomechanics and Constructivism and mark an extreme in Meyerhold's experimentation. After this, Meyerhold began to return to more representational settings, although the self-conscious theatricality of these landmark productions remained in his later repertoire.

THE MEYERHOLD THEATRE (1922–31)

While he worked to achieve a coherent aesthetic on stage, things behind the scenes were anything but stable for Meyerhold. In May 1919, he had been forced out of his job at the Petrograd TEO by a bout of tuberculosis and retired south (to Yalta) to recuperate. The civil war was still in full flight and he was arrested by the Whites, imprisoned and almost executed, three months after leaving Petrograd. A year later he was summoned to return to public life by Lunacharsky and arrived in

Moscow in September 1920. Here, for just over five months, he took overall charge of the theatre department of Lunacharsky's ministry, now covering the whole of the Soviet Union, and launched repeated attacks on the establishment theatres, including the MAT, for their outmoded repertoires and dated style. In late February 1921 he resigned from his position and concentrated his energies on his alternative to the Academic (or state subsidised) theatres – the Russian Soviet Federal Socialist Republic (RSFSR) Theatre No. 1, where he produced the second version of Mayakovsky's *Mystery Bouffe* and a radical adaptation of Emile Verhaeren's *The Dawn*. Ten months after this, on 6 September 1921, the RSFSR theatre was closed and Meyerhold was once again looking for work.

There followed a complex period in which Meyerhold taught his emergent system of biomechanics and began to make public his findings: first, under the auspices of the State Director's Workshop (GVYRM) and then, in January 1922 under the name of GVYTM, the State Theatre Workshop. Later, this second workshop was merged with others under the umbrella of GITIS, the State Institute of Theatrical Art, and it was here where Meyerhold worked most closely with the film maker, Eisenstein. GITIS still exists today, although it is now called the Russian Academy of Theatrical Art, and still has classes in biomechanics, taught by Gennadi Bogdanov, among others. Finally, after breaking away from GITIS, Meyerhold's own workshop was given the name GEKTEMAS (State Experimental Workshop) in 1924.

The theatrical outlets for all this 'laboratory' work were the performances created by Meyerhold's students at the Sohn Theatre – the dilapidated space Meyerhold appropriated in 1922 and which served as his main performance space for almost a decade. During this period, at what became known as the Meyerhold Theatre, the revolutionary director put on some of his most celebrated work, often drawing on the workshop for his casts and achieving a mixture of school, theatre and experimental laboratory that remains an ideal for many directors today. The work in biomechanics did not emerge on the stage directly; the études were never 'quoted' as such, apart from one moment in the *Magnanimous Cuckold*. But the symbiotic relationship of workshop and theatre established by Meyerhold meant that his dramatic productions were always *informed* by the training in biomechanics. This is perhaps most clear in his ground-breaking production of *The Government Inspector* – the most remarkable of his productions from this period.

That story will be told in Chapter 3 and the context surrounding his 1926 production is best described in that section of the book. For now it remains for me to conclude the history of Meyerhold's career by returning to the events with which we began this chapter: the decline of his theatre and his ultimate extermination.

THE DEATH OF MEYERHOLD AND HIS THEATRE (1932–40)

If the 1920s for Meyerhold were characterised by glittering innovation and an immediate responsiveness to things current, then the 1930s would best be described as a period of stagnation. It was a time when Meyerhold (See Figure 1.8) retreated further into the classical repertoire and during which he found it increasingly difficult to practise his craft without intervention or criticism. His range of chosen plays had never been entirely contemporary – the nineteenth-century writers, Gogol, Ostrovsky and Sukhovo-Kobylin, figure prominently in the 'golden age' of his theatre in the previous decade. But these classic playwrights had always been set among the works of new playwrights – Mayakovsky and Erdman, for example – or had themselves been subject to some radical interpretation and/or adaptation. By 1932, the pace of the premières emerging from the Meyerhold Theatre had slowed considerably and the choice of plays was beginning to look dangerously removed from the context of Soviet Russia. Robert Leach lists just eight 'new' productions between 1932 and 1938 (the date when Meyerhold's theatre was finally 'liquidated') and these include revivals of his pre-revolutionary masterpiece *Masquerade* and a return to Griboedov's play *Woe from Wit*, which he had originally staged in 1928 (Leach 1989: 202).

I say 'dangerously' because, increasingly, the presence of Soviet 'censors' was being felt by theatre directors, restricting what new work there was and ensuring that each production toed a party line. The man at the end of that line was Joseph Stalin who, after a bitter internal battle, had taken over from Lenin after his death and from 1928 had taken responsibility for the industrialisation of the country with his first Five Year Plan. By the early 1930s, his control over the party was talked about in terms redolent of Constructivism: he was running a party 'machine', with a well-oiled bureaucracy and a determined aim of productivity. But to keep such productivity going, it was necessary for

Figure 1.8 Meyerhold, 1932

all the separate parts of the machine to work together – to agree – even if that meant compromising the democratic ideals with which the Bolshevik Revolution had begun. This was as true for the arts as it was for agriculture or engineering and in practice it meant a party style: Socialist Realism. All other approaches were denounced as 'formalist', originally a term without prejudice but which became the ultimate condemnation for work which (supposedly) loved itself at the expense of any social message.

Socialist Realism, described by one Russian critic as 'Naturalism without the nature', was defined in 1934 by its key theorist, Andrei Zhdanov, as 'revolutionary romanticism' (Zhdanov *et al.* 1977: 21). It was a style of art which was unflinchingly positive in its presentation of the Revolution and pointedly organised, as Zhdanov puts it, towards 'remould[ing] the mentality of the people in the spirit of socialism' (ibid.: 24).

As such, Socialist Realism sought a response from its audience in direct contrast to that which Meyerhold had been trying to achieve. Meyerhold's ideal was a divided, debating audience. Zhdanov wanted *everybody* to celebrate the successes of the Revolution. The two were bound to come into conflict, all the more so if you consider the absence of any contemporary plays in the repertoire of the Meyerhold Theatre during this period. Meyerhold began to be vilified in the press and accused of formalism. Questions were asked about his current work and about the experiments of the past and he was forced to defend himself from the accusation that his was an 'alien theatre', working against the national cause. One such defence came from Meyerhold in 1936. Using imagery which was tragically prescient, he spoke on the subject of criticism:

> Both as an actor and as a director, my body is so covered in wounds from the critics' shafts that there doesn't seem to be a part left unscathed.
>
> (Braun 1991: 291)

Two years later Meyerhold's theatre was closed, after a final matinée of *The Government Inspector*. For a short time he was adopted by his old mentor, Stanislavsky, and given the job of finishing his opera production *Rigoletto* – Stanislavsky was in the last months of his life. It was a final statement from the teacher that, irrespective of the differences they had experienced over the years, he valued his student's contribution above all.

But this new horizon proved a false one and Meyerhold was arrested on charges of espionage, of plotting to assassinate Stalin and of being part of a counter-revolutionary Trotskyist organisation. The rest we know from the beginning of this chapter. For fifteen years following his execution in 1940 Meyerhold's name was erased from Russian theatre history and his face removed from theatre portraits. His close collaborators were terrified into silence and his acting system, biomechanics, was never mentioned. Only after Stalin was dead did the slow process of rehabilitation begin.

MEYERHOLD TODAY

Fortunately for us, there were people, even in such extreme circumstances, who did not forget Meyerhold and his work. One of these was a young actor called Nikolai Kustov.

Kustov was a collaborator with Meyerhold in the 1930s and taught biomechanics in the same period. Kustov's figure is immortalised in a series of pictures from this time, taken as he performed the actions of the étude 'Shooting the Bow' on a beach (Zarrilli 1995: 94–5), and his work with Meyerhold's biomechanics has similarly defied the passing of time. For Kustov came out of retirement in the 1970s and taught eight actors, working at the Theatre of Satire in Moscow, the art of Meyerhold's biomechanics. By then, he was physically weak and unable to perform the études himself but he nevertheless passed on five of the original études to his actors, two of whom (Gennadi Bogdanov and Aleksei Levinski) are still teaching today.

In doing so, Kustov was defying Stalin's death sentence, keeping alive the spirit of Meyerhold's work, which, for all of the documentary evidence available, nevertheless only truly persists in the body of the actor. What follows is an invitation to continue this process.

2

MEYERHOLD'S KEY WRITINGS

DON'T (ALWAYS) BELIEVE WHAT YOU READ!

Meyerhold's grasp of the finer points of theatre theory was impressive. He was, by any standards, very well read and, if the content of his courses in actor training is anything to go by, he expected his students to develop the same level of sophisticated theatrical understanding. In addition to the practical classes experienced by Meyerhold's students, they were also required to study technical drawing, mathematics, music, social science and the history of world theatres (Hoover 1974: 317–19). Meyerhold's aim is clear to see. He didn't simply require technically able actors. He also wanted well-rounded *thinkers* to graduate from his training school. It must have been a very stimulating, if daunting, environment in which to learn one's craft.

Reading Meyerhold's writings on theatre can also be quite daunting. Edward Braun has made it easier for us by translating them from Russian and by collecting them together in chronological order in the key text *Meyerhold on Theatre* (1991). But there are still complications with Meyerhold's theoretical writings to bear in mind from the outset:

- the writings span more than three decades;
- they come from a wide range of sources;

- they are often written in a deliberately argumentative style;
- they are peppered with a potentially bewildering range of references;
- they are, at times, contradictory.

THIRTY-THREE YEARS OF WRITING

With all of his writings gathered together in one volume it is easy to forget that the range of Meyerhold's thinking is taken from a period lasting nearly thirty-five years, well over half of Meyerhold's life. He began writing for publication in 1906, reflecting on his experience as a junior actor in the Moscow Art Theatre and full of bitter feelings towards Stanislavsky. His last recorded thoughts were given in a speech in 1939, just months before he was executed by Stalin's police. Deprived of his own theatre and, ironically, working at the Stanislavsky Opera, his former teacher is described in this last speech by Meyerhold as 'a mighty phenomenon' (Braun 1991: 299).

Recognise, then, that the writer of 'The Naturalistic Theatre and the Theatre of Mood' (1907), is very different from the author of 'Chaplin and Chaplinism' (1936), even if he bears the same name! This, of course, would be true even if the social and political backdrop to Meyerhold's own life had not shifted at all. But it is difficult to think of a more tumultuous period in history: three revolutions (1905, February and October 1917), one world war, and the shifting of power from one world dictator (Tsar Nicholas II) to another (Joseph Stalin) via a canonised Bolshevik called Lenin.

SOURCES

Unlike Stanislavsky or Michael Chekhov, Meyerhold did not write a book (or books) on acting and, as he began to build his career as a director, he put less and less of his thinking down on paper. In his later years he preferred to let students such as Aleksandr Gladkov (1997) document his thinking for him. As such, Meyerhold's theories have to be sourced from other outlets – transposed lectures, articles, journal contributions, speeches and statements. Consequently, there is no overall design to his theoretical statements, no overarching system. In *An Actor's Work on Himself* Stanislavsky plots the development of a fictional cohort of students over two years of training. You don't have the luxury of such a clear progression when studying Meyerhold's theories.

STYLE

Meyerhold's theoretical work is further complicated by the tone in which some of these articles are written. As a speech-maker or a columnist you have to make your point quickly and efficiently. You can also expect immediate feedback – unlike a book – and so you need to adopt a particular style, one which is sensitive to the immediate critical environment. This is partly true of all writing: nobody operates in a perfect vacuum. But, given the extremity of the circumstances Meyerhold was often operating in, the turbulent first years of the Revolution for example, his thoughts frequently come across with a particularly persuasive vigour. Take his statement on the actor of the future written in 1922:

> An actor working for the new class needs to re-examine all the canons of the past. The very craft of the actor must be completely reorganized.
>
> (Braun 1991: 197)

There are no compromising statements in this kind of writing. It's all or nothing!

The flavour of much of *Meyerhold on Theatre* is, then, *polemical* – it argues for a particular way of thinking which may well be contentious and designed to promote debate. Once one recognises this, it is possible to unpick *how* this rhetoric is being used and thus to probe more deeply into the mind of Meyerhold.

THE RANGE OF REFERENCES

It is not unusual in Meyerhold's writings for him to dazzle his reader with detailed references to writers from across the world, to theatre practitioners of all ages, to painters, composers, philosophers and statesmen, all in the space of a sentence or two! This eclectic range of references gives his writing vibrant colour, but for a new reader, grappling with the ideas themselves, Meyerhold's erudition can be bewildering. Part of the aim of this chapter is to explore the importance of some of these influential figures. But it is as important to adopt a pragmatic editorial eye when reading the primary sources and to recognise that you will not understand all the references Meyerhold makes immediately. Focus on the concepts first (we will be drawing them out here) and then build up your surrounding knowledge of people.

CONTRADICTIONS

It is hardly surprising, given these complexities, that Meyerhold occasionally contradicts himself. Partly, this is a function of writing for over thirty-three years – it is difficult to imagine agreeing with oneself after such a long period. Partly, the contradictions are caused by a shifting political landscape – the Soviet government moved from celebrating experimental work in the 1920s to damning it in the 1930s. But more often than not the contradictions in Meyerhold's work are there for a distinct purpose – to make us *think*. Meyerhold lived a life of contradictions and he integrated his paradoxical existence into his thinking on theatre. Modern politics in this country sometimes make it easy for us to forget that disagreement is not a weakness. Meyerhold reminds us of this fact at every stage.

THE KEY THEORETICAL PRINCIPLES

So, with this health warning in place, we can turn to defining the key areas of Meyerhold's thinking. They are as follows:

- Naturalism *No*
- Stylisation *yell*
- Rhythm and music
- The mask
- The grotesque *p.61*
- Biomechanics and the actor of the future
- Chaplin and Eisenstein: a theory of montage. *p.75*

Whilst there is a kind of chronology implied here – writings from 1906–36 – the guiding principle is to select the elements of Meyerhold's thinking which have a direct relationship to *practice*. For this reason I will amplify some of these concepts with practical ideas and suggested exercises, highlighting that the true worth of *Meyerhold on Theatre* is not to be found in abstract terminology but in *living* theory – in principles which *interweave* with creative practice.

NATURALISM

> Naturalistic Theatre denies the spectator's capacity to fill in the details with his imagination in the way one does when listening to music.
>
> (Braun 1991: 26)

As we have seen in Chapter 1, Meyerhold cut his teeth acting in and directing naturalistic pieces of drama, those which attempted to create an illusion of the 'exact representation of nature' on stage (Braun 1991: 31). His first break as an actor in Stanislavsky's theatre was as Konstantin in Chekhov's *The Seagull* and he went on to play Tuzenbakh in Chekhov's later play, *The Three Sisters*, before being ousted from the company. He maintained a deep respect for the writer of these plays and counted Chekhov's last play, *The Cherry Orchard*, among his favourite of all dramas.

But Meyerhold was no lover of Naturalism as a style. Indeed he spent almost all of his career, after his time at the Moscow Art Theatre, promoting an *anti*-illusionary style of theatre. His first theoretical writings are, in fact, designed to distance himself first from Stanislavsky – whose name became synonymous with Naturalism – and second from what he called the 'absurdities' (ibid.) of the naturalistic project itself.

Thus, Meyerhold begins his theoretical life positioning himself very carefully *against* the dominant style of theatre at the time. He does this in his usual robust and forceful manner. His article 'The Naturalistic Theatre and the Theatre of Mood' (1906) is as much a criticism of his old boss Stanislavsky as it is a tirade against Naturalism as a style. But do not think that this means Meyerhold rejected Naturalism completely or that he learnt nothing from Stanislavsky's theories of theatre. Meyerhold was a highly eclectic director, fusing many different influences together, and the Moscow Art Theatre was far too rich a source of inspiration to be rejected completely.

SEVEN THINGS MEYERHOLD DISLIKED ABOUT NATURALISM

Let's see what Meyerhold found to criticise about Naturalism before considering what he took from his time with Chekhov and Stanislavsky.

First, some words of warning. What Meyerhold is thinking here is highly contentious. He is attacking the MAT – the company who sacked him – at the same time as setting the stage for his own vision, the *stylised* theatre, recorded a year later in 1907. But despite the personal battle Meyerhold was fighting, many of the following criticisms of Naturalism clearly characterise his approach to theatre:

- The emphasis is on trivial detail.
- It leaves nothing to the imagination.
- The actors rely on facial expressions not physical dexterity.
- It results in the actors merely illustrating the playwright's words.
- The natural rhythm of the play is subsumed under surface trivialities.
- The overall shape of the play is lost in the process of textual analysis.
- The naturalistic aim of 'reproducing life on stage' is itself absurd.

We can subdivide these criticisms into two: those related to the actor and those related to the spectator.

THE NATURALISTIC ACTOR

As a director who celebrated the physicality of the actor, Meyerhold's central problem with Naturalism was that it reduced the expressivity of the performer. Instead of using the actor's body to define a character, Naturalism encouraged what Meyerhold called 'reincarnation' (Braun 1991: 24) – a transformation of the actor *into* the character, using make-up, costume and voice. In doing so the actor is encouraged to focus on little details, 'trifles of everyday life' (ibid.: 25), to capture the person they are playing. The kind of performance style Meyerhold was criticising was later to be called 'method mumbling' – an introverted style of acting based on tiny mannerisms, small facial expressions and dialects.

These low-key characters were then placed in a complex and detailed stage environment by the naturalistic director, an environment which for Meyerhold simply echoed the playwright's attempts to create atmosphere. Using sound effects, settings and lighting to reproduce the imaginings of the playwright ran the risk of 'doubling up' the exposition, Meyerhold argued:

> The urge to *show* everything come what may . . . turns the theatre into a mere illustration of the author's words. 'There's the dog howling again', says one of the characters and without fail a dog's howling is reproduced.
>
> (Braun 1991: 30)

Showing 'everything' engages the company in a kind of naturalistic arms race for the ultimately impossible prize: 'reality'. Why invest such effort in attempting to disguise the theatre's own theatricality?, asked Meyerhold. Why not simply give up the pursuit of verisimilitude?

THE NATURALISTIC SPECTATOR

The overwhelming attention to detail in Naturalism denied the spectator their most significant right in the theatre – to *imagine*. Chekhov tells us that everybody leaves offstage and we *believe* him. We don't need to see them being dragged off on a troika at the back of the stage. This was the cardinal error Stanislavsky made in the second version of *The Seagull*, Meyerhold maintained. Once the Art Theatre had the means to produce such effects – in their new theatre – it was sure to exploit the possibilities. But in doing so the MAT was undervaluing the role of the spectators, forcing them out of the creative equation.

The spectator at a naturalistic piece was, as far as Meyerhold was concerned, passive. They were simply being spoon-fed the director's interpretation of the author's words through the agency of the actor. Meyerhold wanted something different. He wanted the spectator and the actor to have equal responsibility in creating the play, to be *co-creators* in the making of a drama.

WHAT DID MEYERHOLD TAKE FROM THE MAT?

At this stage we can't answer this question completely but two interconnected elements do immediately suggest themselves: atmosphere and rhythm.

For Meyerhold, Chekhov was not a naturalistic writer. He was a writer of what he called the 'theatre of mood'. Chekhov *suggested* things in his plays, leaving the audience a good deal of work to do to complete the process. The trick of direction is to facilitate this suggestion, to open up possibilities, not by adding to the atmosphere with further scenic effects but by focusing attention on the 'sheer musicality of the actors' (Braun 1991: 32).

Working on Chekhov's plays taught Meyerhold to search for that musicality – in the rhythm of the language, in the design and in the progression of the scenes. It was a lesson which stayed with him all his life and which clearly informed his writing in the next section on stylisation.

STYLISATION

To maintain that stylisation is an inherent characteristic of art, isn't that the same as defending the thesis that nutritiousness is characteristic of food?

(Gladkov 1997: 99)

Let's begin this section with a practical question: how would you *stylise* a naturalistic scene, say the 'tarantella' scene in Ibsen's *A Doll's House*?

Ibsen's play famously sets Nora, the downtrodden wife or 'doll', against the controlling husband, Torvald Helmer, in what becomes a battle for respect and power. The 'tarantella' scene (Act 2) is a high point in the play where Helmer attempts to choreograph his doll-wife (a symbol of control, of course) in preparation for her performance at a Christmas party:

NORA. Oh, do sit down and play for me, Torvald dear. Correct me, lead the way, the way you always do.

HELMER. Very well, my dear, if you wish it.

[*He sits down at the piano.* NORA *seizes the tambourine and a long multi-coloured shawl from the cardboard box, wraps the shawl hastily around her, then takes a quick leap into the centre of the room and cries.*]

NORA. Play for me! I want to dance!

[HELMER *plays and* NORA *dances.* DR RANK *stands behind* HELMER *at the piano and watches her.*]

HELMER. Slower, slower!

NORA. I can't.

HELMER. Not so violently, Nora.

NORA. I must! . . .

RANK. Let me play for her . . .

[RANK *sits down at the piano and plays.* NORA *dances more and more wildly.* HELMER *has stationed himself by the stove and tries repeatedly to*

correct her, but she seems not to hear him. Her hair works loose and falls
over her shoulders; she ignores it and continues to dance.]

(Ibsen 1980: 77)

Box 2.1

With this extract in mind think about the following two questions:

- What would you need to do in order to perform this piece in the style in which it was originally intended – that is, Naturalism?
- What would you need to do to *stylise* the extract?

(This is best done practically so that you can try your ideas out, but you can begin the process by writing your thoughts down on two separate sheets of paper.)

A NATURALISTIC TARANTELLA

Even if you do not know much about Naturalism, a close reading of the extract gives you some good clues. As a starting point you would need to:

- Cast it: one person for each role: Nora, Helmer and Rank.
- Costume it: perhaps in period costume, with a grand dress for Nora.
- Set it: in a nineteenth-century drawing room!
- Find the props: a piano, a stool, a tambourine, a cardboard box and a shawl.
- Learn the music and the dance for a tarantella.
- Learn the lines as they are recorded in the script.

Once you have done this initial work, you would need to go on to develop the characters, perhaps asking questions about their pasts, their motivations or their particular objectives in this scene. You would be interested to know what happens before this extract and after. And you would have to work hard at ensuring the stage directions are carefully observed, so that, for example, Nora's hair *does* work loose at just the right time.

But there is another way. . . .

A STYLISED TARANTELLA

The term *stylised* is dogged by a history of inaccurate and imprecise use. Too often people describe a production as 'stylised' if it is vaguely non-naturalistic or, worse still, if they are not sure what style it is using at all! For Meyerhold, the verb 'to stylise' meant something very specific and we can understand this if we follow through the work on *A Doll's House*. Meyerhold gives us a clue of what he meant by stylisation in his essay on Naturalism:

> One so often sees overacting in the naturalistic theatre; it knows nothing of the power of suggestion. Yet there were some artists who made use of it, even in the heyday of naturalism: Vera Komissarzhevskaya's Tarantella in *The Doll's House* was no more than a series of expressive poses during which the feet simply tapped out a nervous rhythm.
>
> (Braun 1991: 25)

Although he doesn't say it explicitly at this stage, Meyerhold is describing a process of stylisation. Komissarzhevskaya, his colleague in St Petersburg at the time, has decided not to ape the moves of a famous dance but to simplify the Tarantella into a 'series of expressive poses', underscored by a distinct rhythm. In doing so she has taken three clear steps towards stylisation:

1   to simplify and reduce something down to find its 'essence';
2   to extend the range of expression used;
3   to pay particular attention to the question of rhythm.

SEVEN THINGS MEYERHOLD LIKED ABOUT THE STYLISED THEATRE

- The emphasis is on the actor, working with minimal props and scenery.
- The spectator is compelled to use their imagination.
- The actors rely on physical plasticity and expression.
- The words of the playwright may be transformed by the director.
- Rhythm becomes uppermost in the director's and the spectators' minds.
- The *look* of the work is carefully constructed, like painting a picture.

- The stylised theatre can produce any type of play from Aristophanes to Ibsen.

So, to return to the exercise: you have a free rein with the text, but you need to communicate the *essence* of the scene. You can *reduce* the technical requirements to an absolute minimum. You need to think like a painter and construct the scene with a conscious eye for *form*, *line* and *colour*. Above all, you need to draw on the *physical expressivity* of your performers, concentrating at all times on *rhythm*: the rhythm of the dialogue, the rhythm of the actors' movements, the rhythm of the shapes created when the actors come together in a tableau.

Now take these ideas and *stylise* the extract, putting your stamp on it in the spirit of Meyerhold.

THE RESULTS

There are of course as many ways of stylising this extract as there are directors. But the more successful attempts will have things in common.

They will have thought about the essence of the conflict — perhaps 'a battle of wills', or 'forbidden love', for example. They will have attempted to represent this through largely physical means. They will have been bold with the text, perhaps picking up important phrases and repeating them, or adding pauses. They will have consciously shaped the actors to express the essence of the conflict. They will have been inventive about their use of space and about the choreography of the actors within that space. And they will have found ways of playing with and contrasting the rhythms of the scene. Ultimately, the result should remind us of Meyerhold's stylised production of *Hedda Gabler*, referred to in Chapter 1. The spectator 'may forget the actual words . . . but he cannot forget the overall impression which the scene creates' (Braun 1991: 68).

RHYTHM AND MUSIC

> When human movements become musical even in their form, words will be no more than an embellishment and only fine words will satisfy us.
>
> (Braun 1991: 310–11)

In one sense Meyerhold was closer to the cinema than the theatre in his attitude towards music. Imagine seeing a film without the sound-track. What would it be like? Strange, certainly. At best it would be lacking in atmosphere and tension, and missing that other level of meaning communicated to us through music. A good film score works *with* the action of the movie to create mood, to mark shifts in the film's emotions and to guide the spectator (often unconsciously) towards a particular response. For these reasons Meyerhold considered music to be as fundamental a tool in the theatre director's armoury as it was in the cinemateur's.

But he used it differently. Where a sound score for a film often *confirms* the action on screen, augmenting the mood and manipulating the emotions of the spectator, Meyerhold went against the grain with his theatre music. He was not afraid of giving his audiences conflicting messages and used the clash of music and action to keep them alert and consciously engaged in the performance. He recognised also that, no matter how carefully integrated the music and the action appears for the spectator of a film, this marriage occurs *after* the actors have done their work.

In the theatre it is different – the actors and the music occupy the same space in a live and direct relationship. Meyerhold was keen to exploit this relationship, in his training and in his performances. In doing so he was again distancing himself from the naturalistic theatre and marking his allegiance to the popular theatre – the theatre of the music hall, of melodrama, of circus and pantomime. In these forms music provides a constant stimulus to the action. It is part of the form itself, not simply another layer on top of everything else.

Let's look at music and rhythm in these two areas of his work: training and performance.

TRAINING

The purpose of training is simple: to give the actor the necessary skills for the director to call upon when making a performance. For Meyerhold this meant a wholesale induction into rhythm: 'It's all a question of rhythm of movement and action . . . Rhythm with a capital R' (Braun 1991: 309). Once the actor understands this, he can begin to have a dialogue with the director.

The central rhythm underpinning all Meyerhold's training is made up of three parts. Each part has a name – *otkaz*, *posil'* and *tochka* – and together they constitute the 'abc' of his training method, biomechanics:

- *Otkaz* is the Russian for 'refusal' and describes the preparation an actor makes before any actual action – crouching down before jumping or reaching back before throwing. It's a kind of gestural prologue, if you like.
- *Posil'* (the verb 'to send' in Russian) is the action itself. Sometimes known as the 'realisation', the *posil'* is the actual expression of what was suggested in the prologue, the jump or throw itself.
- *Tochka* marks the end point of a cycle of action. It is the rest at the end of any movement. You might think of it as a kind of frozen epilogue, but an epilogue which always suggests a new start.

The exercises in Chapter 4 will indicate how this tripartite rhythm can be developed in practice, but here the principle of Meyerhold's thinking needs to be understood. Why define such a rhythm for the actor?

1 It gives form and structure to everything you do on stage.
2 It makes explicit any rhythmic choices you might make on stage.
3 It gives freedom within a defined set of boundaries.
4 It establishes a language to be used between actors and with the director.
5 It makes you think in musical terms from the outset.

To illustrate this Box 2.2 (on p. 56) shows a simple task for you to think about.

PERFORMANCE

From his early training as a violinist, Meyerhold was conversant in musical terminology and gained first-hand experience in music-drama, directing works by the German composer Richard Wagner during his time at the Imperial Theatres (1907–17). Meyerhold used music in many of his productions in a number of different ways, collaborating with established composers such as Shostakovich and Gnesin. He even scored his productions like a composer, defining a strict

---

Box 2.2

- Decide upon an action to perform – it might be picking up a glass.
- Now divide this action up into three according to the *otkaz*, *posil'*, *tochka* structure. For example: (a) preparing to pick up the glass, (b) picking up the glass, and (c) returning the glass. (Make sure this finish in some way anticipates more action.)
- Now perform the action again while counting 'and' (for the *otkaz*), 'one' (for the *posil'*) and 'two' (for the *tochka*).
- Try performing the separate actions in an exaggerated physical style.
- Try performing them in a very understated style.
- Have someone look at your action and suggest different rhythms for each part.
- Pair up with someone else and perform a duet – either with the same action again or with something complementary.
- Look back at the five statements in the last paragraph and reflect on the experience.

---

musical structure in his director's notes for *The Lady of the Camellias* (Houghton 1938: 120–1).

Above all, Meyerhold wanted his actors to embody the concept of 'musicality', even if there was no actual music being played. He wanted them to act in the manner of a musical composition: to lend fluidity, contrast, shape and colour to everything they did. There are countless instances of this kind of acting in Meyerhold's work (Chapter 3 will examine one exemplary 'musical' production, *The Government Inspector*, in detail), but a tiny example of one of Meyerhold's greatest actors, Igor Ilinsky, at play is enough to illustrate it here. As Norris Houghton describes:

> In [Chekhov's] *The Proposal* . . . the simple direction, 'He drinks a glass of water,' becomes a small scene. Ilinski breaks off his speech, clutches his heart with one hand, his coat lapel with the other. The father rises, steps back a pace and holds out both his arms, as though Ilinski were about to swim to him. The maid in the background raises her broom and holds it poised in mid-air over her head. There is a pause. The Chopin music begins to play. Ilinski, still

holding his lapel, reaches out with the other hand for the glass on the table. He holds it at arm's length from his mouth; his eyes grow bigger; the music plays louder. The father and maid stand motionless. With a quick jerk Ilinski draws the glass to him and downs the water. The music stops, the maid returns to her sweeping, Ilinski carefully smooths his lapel and returns the glass to the table. The father continues with the next line.

(Houghton 1938: 123)

The Meyerholdian principles of rhythm and musicality are clearly in evidence here. Having done the task of picking up the glass yourself you may already see the structure of Ilinsky's playing. His character, Lomov, a hypochondriac landowner, is defined in this extract by the biomechanical rhythm: *otkaz, posil'* and *tochka*.

First, Ilinsky *prepares* to lift the glass, marking this *otkaz* with a grand gesture across his chest (Lomov suffers from heart palpitations too). He extends this preparation by widening his eyes and lengthening the hold he has on the glass. (All the time the Chopin music underscores the action.) Next, he abruptly *performs* the gesture suggested by the *otkaz*, downing the water in one gulp. Finally, he marks the end of his action (the *tochka*) by smoothing his lapel and returning the glass to the table. The music stops to highlight his conclusive gesture and we assume that his heart will last for a few more minutes at least.

The other two characters respond to the rhythm of his movements, creating a strong sense of ensemble. The father echoes the tension in Ilinsky with his outstretched arms and the maid is frozen in anticipation, before they both resume their original business, the 'turn' having been completed. The overriding impression is of playfulness and of improvisation, but a playfulness that is disciplined by a musical structure and by a shared understanding of rhythm.

THE MASK

The mask may conceal more than just two aspects of a character. . . . How does one reveal this extreme diversity of character to the spectator? With the aid of the mask.

(Braun 1991: 131)

Meyerhold's statement, made in one of his most important essays, 'The Fairground Booth' (published in 1913), captures the equivocality of the mask beautifully. Masks can both conceal and reveal. They are agents of disguise and of disclosure. But one thing, Meyerhold argues, is certain: they are a central part of a spectator's experience.

Let us be clear. When Meyerhold talks of the mask he does not necessarily mean the kind which is made of paper, leather or wood and worn over the face by an actor. Although much of his interest in the mask originates in this kind of object, in *commedia dell'arte* masks for example, his understanding of the mask was more wide-ranging. Masks can be created by make-up, by hairstyle, by facial expressions or by any technique which defines a character in terms of its external characteristics.

And thus the mask can be seen as an overarching metaphor for the type of work Meyerhold wanted to create – a stylised, external, non-psychological, popular theatre.

THE VIRTUES OF THE MASK

I have divided these virtues into three areas: the philosophical, the physical and the theatrical.

Philosophically
- The mask is full of contradictions.
- The mask is both part of history and of 'the moment'.
- The mask constrains and liberates in equal measure.

Physically
- The mask encourages spontaneity, freeing up the expressive work of the actor.
- The mask demands a physical approach to building a character.
- The mask demands clarity of gesture and expression.
- The mask heightens the spectator's awareness of any awkward or unnatural gestures.

Theatrically
- The mask stimulates the imaginations of the audience.
- The mask creates a distance between actor and character.
- The mask can be changed or transformed.
- The mask can show us different perspectives on the same character.

Philosophically speaking, Meyerhold (true to form) enjoyed the mask's paradoxical nature. As we have said, the mask can both reveal or conceal and, depending on how it is manipulated by an actor, it can represent two opposing forces *within the same character*. Meyerhold explains this with reference to the *commedia* figure, Arlecchino, who is both a cheerful (if impoverished) servant and an infernal magician. What is interesting for the audience is to see how these two sides – these two masks within a mask – can inhabit the one character. It is, of course, the physical dexterity of the actor which stimulates the spectator to appreciate this duality – but more of this in a moment.

The other paradoxical aspect of the mask which delighted Meyerhold was its capacity to fuse past and present in one object. The mask of Arlecchino is, Meyerhold argues: 'not only the Arlecchino [the spectator sees] before him but all the Arlecchinos in his memory' (Braun 1991: 131). For Meyerhold, this double life was fundamental. The intrinsic power of the mask to live in the memory and in the moment at the same time echoed his own practice; his own consistent attempt to marry tradition and innovation. In this way Meyerhold managed to resolve some of the key tensions in his work, particularly after the Revolution. Looking back to the traditions of an older, popular theatre was not, as some maintained, a retrogressive move for Meyerhold, but a way of delivering a specific kind of modernity.

Physically, the mask makes great demands on an actor. Again it has a strange duality. On the one hand it is something comforting to hide behind, something which can release inhibitions. On the other, it is an impassive indicator of your weaknesses. For Meyerhold, most important was the way in which the mask forces the actor to externalise his means of communication – to use the body.

This is true whether one is wearing an actual mask or creating one. The shapes generated by the body need to complement the expression of the face. If there are distinct facial characteristics, if the mask is especially angular or rotund, the body can echo this. Also, the gestures must not be overly complex or confusing for an audience. There must be a simple clarity in everything the actor/mask does. In short, the mask must: '*Show* (not "tell") the audience what it is seeing, and it has to do so with the whole body' (Frost and Yarrow 1990: 123).

This concept of 'showing' brings me on to the question of theatricality. Firstly and most crucially, the mask demands a particular relationship to the audience – a direct, full-frontal playing style. There

(Charlie Chaplin)

is no point in seeing the side of a m⟨...⟩ ⟨...⟩r's
head. Masks operate forwards. ⟨...⟩ry
between stage and spectator, ⟨...⟩r
dimmed auditoria. Indeed, the ⟨...⟩t
feedback from the audience. Mas⟨...⟩
naturalistic. It is a *stylised* form, ch⟨...⟩
on an audience's *imagination* – a k⟨...⟩
of stylisation. 'Is it not the mask,' ⟨...⟩ airground
Booth', 'which helps the spectator fl⟨...⟩ ⟨...⟩ land of make-believe'
(Braun 1991: 131).

So mask does not demand presence

This outward quality of the mask in performance is of course
theatrical in itself. The character is 'presented', or 'shown', to the
audience – verbs which already indicate a level of distance between
actor and character. Masks can, in addition, be changed and thus one
character can be exposed to an audience from a number of different
perspectives. This heightens our feeling of theatricality still further and
encourages us to view the character in terms of *how* they are constructed. Multiple masks can in fact lay bare the underlying processes
of theatre-making, processes which the world of Naturalism would
deny even existed.

Meyerhold's understanding of character reflects this view of the
mask. Seek out the contradictions, the contrasts, the conflicts in your
character, he instructed, then illustrate those differences in physical
terms. *Construct* your characters from the outside in, scoring their
progress through the play in discrete 'turns' or events.

The result was what one might call a 'character/montage', the kind
Erast Garin, one of Meyerhold's favourite actors, created for the part
of Khlestakov in *The Government Inspector*:

> In different scenes he played the mask of the dandy, the mask of the liar, the
> mask of the glutton, the mask of the opportunist – a grotesque gallery in other
> words, centred on Garin's spindly physique. However, the fact that each
> scene had its own mask enabled the actor to remain emotionally detached
> from the part as such and to display a range of ironic comments on the char-
> acter he was playing. Garin himself pointed out that the actor must be
> technically equipped to do this, and insisted that his technique had been
> developed through the exercises in biomechanics he had had in the Meyerhold
> workshop.

(Leach 1989: 76–7)

This description of Garin's Khlestakov takes us back and forward at the same time. The multiple masks capture clearly one of the ideas discussed in this section: Meyerhold's fluid and expressive approach to building character. The effect of this approach, however – Garin's '*grotesque* gallery' – begs further questions: in particular an investigation of the term 'grotesque', arguably one the most significant of all the words commonly associated with Meyerhold.

THE GROTESQUE

> In handling the grotesque, the artist attempts to cause the spectator to suddenly pass from a plane with which he is familiar, to another plane which is unexpected.
>
> (Symons 1971: 67)

Meyerhold hated anything predictable, especially in the theatre. Predictability breeds comfort which soon becomes boredom, and both are the kiss of death for a theatre director. For this reason Meyerhold turned to the grotesque, the genre of surprise, about which he said:

> The grotesque isn't something mysterious. It's simply a theatrical style which plays with sharp contradictions and produces a constant shift in the planes of perception.
>
> (Gladkov 1997: 142)

'Contradiction' is once more to be found at the heart of Meyerhold's thinking and once more its function is to unsettle the audience. If predictability leads to comfort then the grotesque breeds its opposite, discomfort, by encompassing the following unsettling qualities:

- It mixes opposites: tragedy and comedy, life and death, beauty and ugliness.
- It celebrates incongruities.
- It challenges our perceptions.
- It is naturally mischievous, even satirical.
- It borrows from different (and unlikely) sources.
- It always has a touch of the diabolical, the devil's influence.
- It stretches the natural to the extent that it becomes *un*natural or stylised.

- It revels in fantasy and mystery.
- It is constantly transforming things: objects, figures, landscapes and atmospheres.

As with many of his statements on the mask, Meyerhold's central ideas of the grotesque hail from the essay 'The Fairground Booth' – after Aleksandr Blok's play of the same name. Characteristically, this essay draws on many sources. In fact, in the space of just five pages Meyerhold has cause to refer to no fewer than sixteen artists, all of whom have used the grotesque in their work. But of these sixteen, there are three key people whose work exemplifies the characteristics listed above better than any others: Goya, Hoffmann and Blok. Painter, novelist and playwright respectively, these three artists were favourites of Meyerhold's and offer vibrant and stimulating examples of the grotesque at work. Let's take them in reverse order.

ALEKSANDR BLOK

We have already encountered Aleksandr Blok and his grotesque play in some detail in Chapter 1. But let me briefly remind you of the facts: Meyerhold directed and acted in Blok's *The Fairground Booth* in 1906 in Vera Komissarzhevskaya's theatre in St Petersburg; Blok based his play on characters from *commedia dell'arte*, including Arlecchino (or Harlequin) and Columbine, with Meyerhold himself playing Pierrot; and despite being a symbolist writer, Blok satirises the movement of Symbolism with his chorus of Mystics, retaining a critical detachment throughout.

Blok's play is a lively, playful and extravagant romp based on a love triangle. Just ten pages long, it is packed full of grotesque delights and leaps from one heightened theatrical moment to another. Take a look at the stage direction below and see if you can identify any of those unsettling characteristics of the grotesque:

> [*One of the clowns takes it into his head to play a prank. He runs up to the* LOVER *and sticks out a long tongue at him. The* LOVER *brings his heavy wooden sword down on the* CLOWN's *head with all his might. The* CLOWN *is doubled over the footlights, where he remains hanging. A stream of cranberry juice gushes from his head.*]
>
> CLOWN [*in a piercing yell*]. Help! I'm bleeding cranberry juice!

[*Having dangled there for a while, he gets up and goes out. Uproar.*
Confusion. Gleeful shouts: 'Torches! Torches! A torchlight procession!'
Members of the chorus appear, carrying torches. Maskers throng, laughing
and leaping about.]

(Green 1986: 55)

Blok's grotesque mixing of opposites should be very clear here. The
clown breaks up a pair of lovers with a mischievous prank, sticking an
enlarged tongue out at the assembled pair. What was a romantic
exchange is thus transformed by the interruption of a comedian. The
scene then shifts almost immediately to what looks to be a tragic
murder, the clown draped over the footlights, bleeding from a fatal
wound in his head. But although the clown shrieks in pain, the weapon
which caused the injury is clearly a prop – a wooden sword – and the
blood which is spurting from the gash is, by his own admission, only
cranberry juice. His theatrical death throes are then abruptly curtailed
as he decides to exit the stage, leaving a confused atmospheric mixture
of glee and anger.

We're not sure whether to laugh or cry in this situation (although
an unmistakable carnivalesque feeling is implied by the arrival of
the dancing maskers). What is clear is that Blok's style is not afraid
of collisions, transformations and surprises – a model, in fact, of the
grotesque.

E.T.A. HOFFMANN

In one sense Hoffmann (1776–1882) follows on naturally from Blok,
for it was shortly after Meyerhold's staging of Blok's *The Fairground
Booth* that he moved to the Imperial Theatre in St Petersburg and to his
double life under the Hoffmann-inspired pseudonym of Dr Dapertutto.
(Dapertutto was a character in Hoffman's *Adventure on New Year's Eve*
who, like Meyerhold in this period, led a mysterious double life.)

In fact, Hoffmann himself was two very different people in one body.
A lawyer by day, he transformed himself into a fantasy writer in the
evenings, creating works of dark and haunting beauty, and it was clearly
this enigmatic duality which appealed to Meyerhold. Hoffmann's stories
are notable for their interweaving of dream and reality, for their fluid
transformations and for their use of startling images of incongruity. In
Meyerhold's own words:

> The grotesque mixes opposites, consciously creating harsh incongruity and
> relying solely on its own originality. In Hoffmann, ghosts take stomach pills, a
> bunch of flaming lilies turns into [a] gaudy dressing gown ... the student
> Anselmus is fitted into a glass bottle.
>
> (Braun 1991: 138)

These are highly *theatrical*, as well as beautiful literary images, inviting
a director to stretch his imagination to the limit. They also encapsulate
the idea of 'strangeness', a strangeness born of mixing things in unusual
ways. The result, as Meyerhold says, is 'original', not because the individual ingredients are strange necessarily, but because the mix itself is
unique. What Meyerhold saw in Hoffmann was an ideal mode of
creative thinking. His stories are, in effect, a paradigm for the theatre
director, a rallying cry for the power of the imagination.

To illustrate this last point, have a look at the following extract from
one of Hoffmann's short stories – *The Mines at Falun* (1819) – and
imagine how you, as a director, might stage the moment. You might
also look again for the hallmarks of the grotesque:

> Hardly had he [Elis] stretched out on his bed, worn out and weary as he was,
> when dreams touched him with their wings. It seemed as if he were floating in
> a ship under full sail on a mirror bright sea with a vault of dark clouds above
> him. Yet as he looked down into the water, he realized that what he had taken
> for the sea was a solid transparent sparkling mass into whose shimmering
> light the whole ship dissolved away, so that he was standing on a crystalline
> floor and above him was a vault of glittering black rock. ... Propelled by
> an unknown power, he took a step forward, but at that instant everything
> around him stirred, and there arose from the ground like rippling waves strange
> flowers and plants of flashing metal. ... Soon, his gaze penetrating deeper, he
> saw at the very bottom countless lovely maidens embracing one another with
> white shining arms. ... An indescribable feeling of pleasure and pain seized
> the youth.
>
> (Hoffmann 1982: 317–18)

What a wonderful challenge Hoffmann sets us: how to reproduce
the constantly shifting landscape of Elis's dream. Clearly, the answer
lies in finding an expressive, stylised approach, for Hoffmann's visions
take us instantaneously from the realm of normality – Elis's room –
to a rich world of fantasy. Also significant is the youth's emotional

reaction. He is caught between two extremes, between pleasure and pain, between the dark rocks and the glittering white maidens. It is precisely this kind of unsettling mixture which Meyerhold sought to create in his own work.

FRANCISCO GOYA

Meyerhold often looked to visual stimuli when preparing a production. His own pictorial imagination was highly developed, but he recognised that there were many other sources to stimulate his thinking and one of those was the Spanish painter and printmaker, Goya (1746–1828). Goya is matched with Hoffmann in Meyerhold's mind for his satirical bite, for his depiction of wild fantasies and for the blending of oppositional elements. The Spanish artist subjects countless figures to his scorn: gentlemen, politicians, the clergy, parents, teachers, artists. And as such he represented something central to Meyerhold – that the power structures of the world can be opened up to scrutiny using an extended and vibrantly expressive style.

To get a sense of this style it is a good idea to look at the range of Goya's prints (see Pérez Sánchez and Gállego 1995). For it is in his print work, more so than in his paintings with oil, that he finds a specific clarity of expression. Using just black and white, and the most delicate attention to line and form, Goya creates vivid atmospheres, characters and emotions – essential ingredients for the theatre as well. Very

---

Box 2.3

Take a look at the example, entitled *The Sleep of Reason Produces Monsters* (see Figure 2.1). Make notes on the following:

- What you think is the overall meaning of the piece.
- How Goya has focused our attention using light and dark (chiaroscuro).
- How Goya has combined opposites, for example the symbols of reason against the images of monsters or demons.
- What steps the artist has taken to represent two worlds – the natural and the supernatural, or the conscious and the unconscious.
- What feelings the print inspires in you.

Figure 2.1 Francisco Goya's *The Sleep of Reason Produces Monsters*, 1797

quickly you will begin to understand the impact of these works with their distorted faces, fantastic vistas and grotesque combinations. Again, like Hoffmann, these images are a challenge to the mind. They represent the power of the grotesque to be simultaneously tragic and comic but always with a serious intent.

If, like me, you answered the final question with the word 'mixed', then Goya's grotesque art has succeeded. For inscribed within this curious etching are many unsettling and yet intriguing elements. We are drawn to the central figure of the author. We recognise the toil of his creative efforts and note how well presented he is with frock coat and breeches. But in the background – in the other world of the picture – is a very different vision, a chilling insight into his own disturbed mind. Simultaneously the source and the victim of these harpy-like owls, the author is clearly an equivocal figure, reminding us perhaps of Hoffmann or his character, Dapertutto.

We are, in effect, forced to see the realistic figure of the author in a new light; forced, in fact, to shift our attention to a new, unexpected plane. Hence, we return to Meyerhold's opening definition of the grotesque. The normal has been 'made strange' by the power of an artist's vision.

BIOMECHANICS AND THE ACTOR OF THE FUTURE

Biomechanical training might be compared to a pianist's studies. . . . Mastering the technical difficulties of the exercises and études does not provide the student with a prescription for the lyric energy necessary, let's say, to perform a Chopin nocturne . . . yet he must master the techniques in order to master his art. Technique arms the imagination.

(Schmidt 1996: 41)

The words are Garin's, one of Meyerhold's most talented actors, and they make beautifully clear the place of Meyerhold's training in his theatre. Biomechanics, invented by Meyerhold roughly between 1913 and 1922, develops the actor's underlying technical discipline. It is the bread and butter work he does in order to master his art. But the training is only half of the equation. Once the actor has mastered his own material, he can go on to use his technical ability in the pursuit of art. You never see a pianist practising his scales in a concert hall. But you know the beauty of their playing is the product of thousands of hours of practice. In the same way, the physical forms of biomechanics – the études – are not to be seen on stage, but they nevertheless inform everything the actor does in front of the audience.

The dates above are significant because they straddle that all-important moment in Russian history, 1917 – the year of the Revolution. Consequently, the language used to describe biomechanics is inextricably caught up with the language of the Revolution. It is not simplifying the matter too much to say that Meyerhold's key influences before the Revolution were *theatrical*. But these sources are coloured after 1917 by two other areas of influence: the *industrial* and the *psychological*. The result is a complex synthesis of ideas which are crystallised in the actor's work on the biomechanical études.

THEATRICAL INFLUENCES

Meyerhold's first formal acting studio was founded in 1913. The curriculum was divided into three classes, which give us a good clue as to the theatrical priorities of the studio:

1 *Commedia dell'arte*
2 Musical reading
3 Movement on stage.

Meyerhold's collaborator, Solovyov, took the *commedia* class, which involved exercises in so-called 'antics appropriate to the theatre'. These were skills involving acrobatics, the play with props, engaging the audience and physicalising a scenario. The future composer for Meyerhold's production of *The Government Inspector*, Mikhail Gnesin, led the classes in music, concentrating on the rhythmic aspects of text, specifically in ancient Greek drama. And Meyerhold himself took the movement class, justifying in practice his theoretical maxim: 'Movement is the most powerful means of theatrical expression' (Braun 1991: 147).

Meyerhold's class in movement was characteristically eclectic, drawing on as wide a range of practical sources as we have seen him use in his theoretical treatises. He divided his class into two: an 'actors class' and a 'grotesque group' with the former taking on work in the same tradition as *commedia* and the latter working on their own plays. One exercise undertaken by the grotesque group at the invitation of

Filippo Marinetti (the futurist playwright and theorist) sums up the physical bias of the work. You can attempt this yourself and record your feelings about the exercise.

Box 2.4

- Get into a group of four (although any size, including solos, is equally good).
- Decide upon a Shakespeare play with which you are familiar (you don't have to know it inside out).
- Start the stopwatch.
- Spend *three minutes* recalling the main events of the whole play.
- Perform a *three-minute version* of your edited play.
- Reflect on the choices made.

Marinetti asked Meyerhold's class to work on *Othello*, but the results will be similar in any case. Here's what the student playing Iago said after the exercise:

> I knelt to pick up the handkerchief Desdemona had lost, followed her with my eyes and looked again at the handkerchief. . . . I then waved the handkerchief before Othello, who seized it.

(Hoover 1974: 83)

You may well have found the same kind of moments in your version: physically explicit gestures which summarise *the essence* of the play (in this instance the jealousy of Othello) without the need for lengthy speeches. The exercise effectively forces you to externalise the text, to think of it in pictorial or emblematic terms and to strip it of any subtext or embellishments. In fact, what you are creating is the beginning of an étude.

INDUSTRIAL INFLUENCES

With a deposed aristocracy and a failing economy, priorities shifted considerably after the Revolution. The new buzzwords were 'efficiency', 'productivity' and 'collectivity', with the country united in an

effort to drag itself into the twentieth centur two decades after
everyone else. But, in a strange way, these ases, in what was
now a *Soviet* culture, did not take Me cally away from
his declared theatrical objective his *language*.
Writing in 1922, a year aft g studio was
opened, the voice of

> The methods of Tay the same
> way as they are to an produc-
> tivity.

(Braun 1991: 198)

But when you look deeper in or of the future', the same key
theatrical concerns prevail. The or may now need to be conversant
in the laws of mechanics and of proxemics (space), but this knowledge,
even if it is expressed in new 'scientific terms', keys into identical priorities for the performer: the need for precision, for coordination and for
clarity of expression; and the requirement that an actor has rhythmic
understanding and is responsive and disciplined.

Rather than citing the popular tradition of theatre as an exemplar of
this kind of work, Meyerhold now turned his sights to contemporary
figures of esteem. Not the tragedies of Shakespeare, but the 'scientific
management' of Taylor; no longer the *commedia* of Gozzi, but the
factories of Gastev, Taylor's emissary in Russia.

Frederick Winslow Taylor (1856–1915) was an American industrialist who pioneered the use of 'time and motion' studies in the
workplace. His ultimate aim was to pare down the complex actions
encountered by workers in factories to a series of connected *tasks*. He
gave each of these tasks a maximum time in which they could be
completed, so that when these component parts of the job were
performed together, the total time for the action was reduced quite
dramatically.

The best way to think of this is to *Taylorise* an action you do yourself, break it down into its constituent parts. Let's take 'making
breakfast'. What are the constituent actions for assembling the first
meal of the day? They could be:

1 Open the kitchen door
2 Walk to the cupboard

3   Open the cupboard door
4   Get a bowl from the cupboard
5   Close the cupboard door
6   Walk to the cereal cupboard
7   Open the cupboard door
    And so on. . . .

Immediately it becomes clear that a simple job is made up of many separate actions or tasks and the time it takes for each one of these actions to be performed may be longer than is *absolutely necessary*. There are two responses to this eventuality: (1) rationalise the job itself or (2) speed up the individual actions by performing them more efficiently. In the first instance, time can be spared quickly: keep the cereal with the bowls and you halve the number of actions! But once this rationalisation has been done, the actions themselves need to be carried out more effectively. So how is this done?

It is at this point that Meyerhold's key priorities come back into play, now expressed through the language of the industrialist, but strangely redolent of the generic skills identified before the Revolution. A skilled worker, the new model for the theatre, exhibits the following characteristics:

1) an absence of superfluous, unproductive movements; 2) rhythm; 3) the correct positioning of the body's centre of gravity; 4) stability.

(Braun 1991: 198)

Indeed, the factory worker's toil, Meyerhold argues, 'borders on art' (ibid.) in its dance-like fluidity. Earlier, it was the *commedia* actor who exhibited such ability, but the skills remain the same. Before we go on to analyse how this 'new' language of industry impacts on the étude work, let's turn to the final piece in the jigsaw, psychology.

PSYCHOLOGICAL INFLUENCES

The native Russian figure to be internationally celebrated at the time was the objective psychologist, Ivan Pavlov (1849–1936). Pavlov is most famous for his theories of *reflexology:* a theory of the mind based on the premise that we can only understand what we can *objectively* measure, that is, physical processes, not subjective moods. This premise led Pavlov to work on animals, and specifically to measuring the salivation levels in dogs in response to different stimuli.

Emerging from this work was Pavlov's central theory: that animal behaviour (including that of humankind) is best understood in terms of *reflexes*. It might be a tap on the knee or the ringing of a bell, but in either case there is no *volitional* process at work in our response. We don't, in other words, make choices, we simply respond to things outside of us. Animals are, in effect, rather like machines: we don't act, we *re*act, in response to an external stimulus. Pavlov's theory suggested that these reflexes join together in long chains of actions and reactions – a kind of domino line of reflexes which, at the largest scale, constitutes our very existence.

Pavlov's theory was very popular in post-revolutionary Russia, not least because its emphasis was on the external, material aspects of life. These were things which could be consciously manipulated, unlike the unknown forces of the 'unconscious'.

It all seems a far cry from the world of acting. For Meyerhold, though, Pavlov's theory accorded with his own objective view of the actor, his emphasis on external physicality. Again, the language he uses to describe this kind of actor is carefully chosen:

> An actor must posses the capacity for *Reflex Excitability*. Nobody can become an actor without it.

And:

> From a sequence of physical positions and situations there arise *points of excitation* which are informed with some particular emotion.
>
> (Braun 1991: 199–201)

Emotion, he maintained, does not comes from the inner workings of the mind but from an outside stimulus, from 'physical positions and situations'. Emotion is, in effect, a reflex.

BIOMECHANICS: A SYNTHESIS OF THE THEATRICAL, INDUSTRIAL AND PSYCHOLOGICAL

The big question remains. How did these unusual influences come together in the practical work of the actor? In creating the biomechanical études, Meyerhold drew on the following ideas: the physical dexterity and playfulness of the popular theatre, including *commedia*; presenting the essence of a story in a short physical performance; dividing up an action into a number of efficiently performed tasks; and connecting those tasks in a long chain of reflexes.

He effectively synthesised the *form* of Taylor and Pavlov with the *content* of *commedia* to produce a set of études designed to address all the basic skills of the actor. You will have a chance practically to experience this creative fusion in Chapter 4, where all the basic skills are outlined and one étude – 'The Slap' – is discussed in detail.

Box 2.5

As a taster to that chapter consider the following:

- How might you break down a comic piece of stage business such as a slap into its constituent parts?
- How might you connect these actions to tell the essence of the story?
- How might you work on each single action to eradicate anything superfluous?
- How might you embody the mechanical principles of rhythm, efficiency, stability and stamina?
- How might you perform these actions as if they are a reflex?

CHAPLIN AND EISENSTEIN: A THEORY OF MONTAGE

> Quiet field
> Butterfly flying
> Sleeping.
> (Eisenstein 1988: 140)

Take a moment to think about what is in your head after reading this Japanese *haiku*, or short song: images, feelings, colours, perhaps even smells or textures, all evoked by just five words. What is it that makes us respond so readily?

MONTAGE

According to Eisenstein, Meyerhold's former pupil and key proponent of the theory, montage involves:

> The simplest juxtaposition of two or three details of a material series, produc[ing] a perfectly finished representation of another order, the psychological.
>
> (Eisenstein 1988: 140)

Put two different things together, one after the other, and our *psychological* response to those things is to create a third 'representation', a higher level of meaning produced by our own skills of association. Eisenstein gives us some examples of this process in a different essay:

Eye + Water = Crying   Door + Ear = Eavesdropping

Child + Mouth = Screaming   Knife + Heart = Anxiety

(1988: 164)

The two objects collide with each other and, in his own words, 'explode' (ibid.) into a concept.

THREE GOOD REASONS FOR CONCLUDING WITH CHAPLIN AND EISENSTEIN

So what does this have to do with Meyerhold? And why are we concluding with a section dedicated to film theory and not the theatre? (Both Eisenstein and Chaplin were first and foremost film-makers, after all.)

First, because both men are referred to in one of the last essays penned by Meyerhold: 'Chaplin and Chaplinism' (1936). It therefore marks the end of our journey through Meyerhold's theories.

Second, because the theory of montage is as important for an understanding of theatre as it is to film. Indeed, without a rudimentary introduction to montage, Meyerhold's adaptation of *The Government Inspector* (the subject of the next chapter) would be difficult to understand fully.

Third, and most importantly, what Meyerhold has to say about Chaplin in particular is true of all great biomechanical actors, even if Chaplin himself didn't train in biomechanics. He was a natural performer in the Meyerholdian style, 'a master' (Braun 1991: 314) in Meyerhold's own words, and all of his great work has endured for us to examine and enjoy today. (Less than two minutes of any contemporary footage of Meyerhold's actors has survived.)

MONTAGE IN THE THEATRE

Before we go on to examine Chaplin's mastery, let's outline what a theory of montage means for the theatre director:

- An *episodic* structure to the overall production.
- Carefully directed juxtaposing of the episodes to maximise the 'explosive' effect.
- Surprises, collisions, incongruities.
- Pronounced and varying *rhythms* emerging from the overall montage.
- A *thinking* audience, putting together the meaning for itself.
- The possibility of two or more parallel storylines.
- A clear sense of theatricality, of being aware of the joins in the montage.

Thus, Meyerhold's use of montage brings a number of other elements of this chapter together. An episodic structure works against the incremental progression of Naturalism. It therefore supports all manner of *stylisation*. Montage is intrinsically *musical*: the arrangement of the overall production can be likened to a composition. In Robert Leach's words: 'each brick or "turn" is a rhythmic element, and the composition is thus fundamentally a rhythmic construction' (1989: 122). The collisions of ideas generated by montage naturally lead to the mixing of opposites and hence to the *grotesque*. And the Montage itself is facilitated by the view of character as inconsistent or fluid, the result one might say of multiple *masks* in performance.

CHAPLIN AS MASTER

The same synthesising function may also be attributed to Chaplin, which could explain his elevated place in Meyerhold's thinking. Chaplin's work as an actor and a director does, in fact, incorporate many of the key concepts expounded in this chapter, as well as raising one or two other issues. Meyerhold saw in Chaplin the same:

- authorial attitude – both he and Chaplin considered themselves to be the ultimate creators of the work;
- commitment to forging an ensemble ethic in his company;
- belief in art as a tool for social criticism;
- ability to mix tragedy and comedy;
- encouragement of an audience to make associations through montage.

Above all, Meyerhold celebrates in this last essay the ability of Chaplin naturally to embody the principles of biomechanics. 'The object of our experiments' in biomechanics, Meyerhold states unequivocally, 'was the maximum exploitation of the expressive power of movement. This skill can be acquired from a study of Chaplin' (Braun 1991: 321).

As a final task for this chapter then, let me invite you to begin that study, specifically to watch the opening moments of the film Meyerhold called a 'monumental canvas' (ibid.: 314): *Modern Times* (1936). Keep an eye out for Chaplin's:

- use of montage as a director, cutting from sheep to factory workers;
- careful exposure of the hierarchies in the workplace – manager, under-manager, supervisor, worker;
- incredible timing and rhythmic awareness at work on the conveyor belt;
- use of the mask, drawn from his observation of reality, but extended and made his own;
- integration of music and action;
- physical precision, balance and expressiveness;
- punctuation of the action with stillness, those 'momentary pauses for aim' (Braun 1991: 321).

And don't forget to laugh!

3

MEYERHOLD'S KEY PRODUCTION

The Government Inspector

GOGOL'S CHALLENGE

Think of yourself as a director for a moment. You have Nikolai Gogol's nineteenth-century comedy, *The Government Inspector* (1836), in your hands and you are looking at the final page. Here's Gogol's extended stage direction, the moment with which he concludes his play:

> *The* MAYOR *stands in the centre, like a pillar, with his arms outstretched and his head flung back. To the right are his* WIFE *and* DAUGHTER, *their entire bodies straining towards him; behind them stands the* POSTMASTER, *transformed into a sort of question mark, facing the audience; behind him stands the* SCHOOLS SUPERINTENDENT, *with a look of helpless innocence; behind him and at the far side of the stage, three visiting ladies, leaning against one another with the most satirical expression on their faces, are looking straight at the* MAYOR's *family. To the left of the* MAYOR *stands the* CHARITIES WARDEN, *his head cocked to one side as if straining to listen; behind him the* JUDGE, *with his arms stuck out, is practically squatting on the floor, and moving his lips, as if trying to whistle. . . . Behind him,* KOROBKIN, *facing the audience with his eyes screwed up, directs a look of contempt at the* MAYOR; *and behind him again, at the other side of the stage, stand* BOBCHINSKY *and* DOBCHINSKY, *their arms outflung towards each other, open-mouthed and goggle-eyed. The other guests stand around like pillars. The petrified company maintain their position for almost a minute and a half. Then the curtain is lowered.*

(Gogol 1997: 100)

You may well be asking yourself: 'How on earth am I going to do that?'. How am I going to capture the audience's attention for a full ninety seconds, as they watch a frozen dumb show of 'petrified' characters?

Now ask your next question as a director: what does this conclusion tell me about Gogol's theatrical vision? Why does he ask so much of an audience at this critical moment in the play? As a skilled dramatist, Gogol would be well aware of the dangers of this finale: losing the audience's attention, leaving them on a low point, or worse still inviting them to point out any flaws in the quality of the actors' freeze. But he knew, too, the impact that such a moment could make if it were successfully realised on stage, how electrifying such unabashed theatricality could be in the hands of a master director.

In effect, Gogol is challenging the director to ask themselves the question: Do I have sufficient creative, imaginative and performative resources within my company to stage this piece?

MEYERHOLD'S RESPONSE

By the time Meyerhold attempted to direct Gogol's play in 1926, he had built himself a considerable reputation for meeting such theatrical challenges. From his early days on tour with the Fellowship, through the double life he led in St Petersburg, to the founding of his own theatre in Moscow, he had staged well over 100 productions, and proved himself to be an exceptionally versatile director.

But of all his productions, Meyerhold's response to the challenge of *The Government Inspector* (*Revisor* in Russian) was particularly remarkable. There are many reasons for this, most of which I hope will be highlighted in this chapter. But one central reason needs stressing from the outset: Gogol's play was tailor-made for Meyerhold's theatre. If you look back to the stage direction above, you can see why. This incredible *coup-de-théâtre* incorporates many of the devices we have already encountered in Meyerhold's work:

- The deliberate choreography of the characters within the stage space.
- The sense of the stage as a picture or composition.
- The use of an exaggerated and expressive physical style.
- The use of the face as a mask.
- The mixing of opposites.

- The direct connection with an audience.
- The elongation of an action to make it strange.

With such a stylistic meeting of minds it was only a matter of time before Meyerhold took on Gogol's classic text, for *The Government Inspector* was the ultimate test of how his theories combined with his practice.

It is for this reason that his production is so worthy of another look. It is a measure of how well Meyerhold managed to synthesise his ideas into one performance. What's more, it is relatively easy to find material to make this judgement. In addition to the original source (Gogol's play), a whole host of people have documented their responses to Meyerhold's 1926 production – actors, theatre critics, academics, politicians – so there are several resources we can turn to in fleshing out our understanding of the work.

One key objective for this chapter must be to place Nikolai Gogol in context, to draw out his intentions as a playwright, and to summarise the contents of the play itself. But my overriding aim is to use Meyerhold's production to exemplify this meeting point between theory (the subject of the last chapter) and practice (the topic of the next). A production is one of the most powerful indicators of how a practitioner's thinking and training come together. It is where creativity meets with hard graft, where technique confronts the imagination, and where abstract thought informs concrete actions. For this reason I have punctuated the material of this chapter with some practical suggestions of how to draw on Gogol's text in the spirit of Meyerhold. This chapter may be treated as a precursor to the next, or it might be returned to after reading up on what Meyerhold asked of his actors in the studio. Either way, Meyerhold's theory and practice are best thought of as two halves of a complex and creative equation called 'performance', not as separate activities.

So how did Meyerhold managed to stage this amazing ending? Konstantin Rudnitsky, one of the most important commentators on Meyerhold, offers this description:

> The curtain rose, and the spectators saw the characters of the show frozen in the poses indicated by Gogol. The sculptural group was immobile. Only after a long pause did the spectators guess that before them were not actors but dolls – that the 'mute scene' was truly mute and dead.
>
> (Rudnitsky 1981: 417–18)

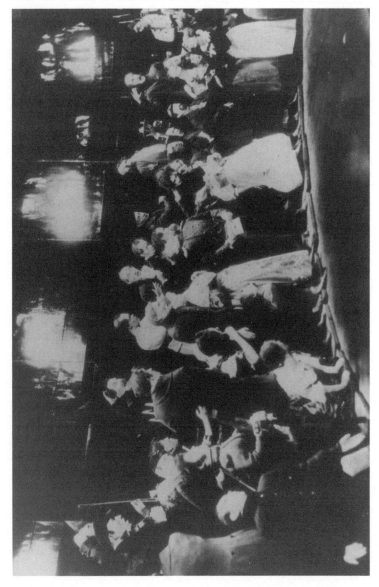

Figure 3.1
Meyerhold's
*Government
Inspector:*
'Dumbshow',
1926

Meyerhold's response to the challenge set by Gogol exactly ninety years earlier was characteristically imaginative: substitute mannequins for the actors in the blink of an eye and Gogol's metaphor of petrification is transformed into a concrete image on stage (see Figure 3.1). What's more, if you can perform it with such a theatrical sleight of hand that the assembled audience are fooled, then they too will be drawn into the silent moment, made mute by the miraculous appearance of puppets. This was Meyerhold's answer to Gogol. He gulled his audience into believing that the cast were still on stage and then pulled the rug from beneath them. Surprise, surprise!

But who are these people who turn to stone in front of your eyes? Why are they moved to such hysteria? And what has the Mayor done which makes him the focus of everything? More fundamentally, who created these characters? Who is Nikolai Gogol? And where does he fit into Russian theatre history? Once we have established these facts, we can return to Meyerhold's production of Gogol's play and to the task in hand – a practical exposition of what has frequently been called Meyerhold's 'masterpiece', one of the landmark productions of the twentieth century.

NIKOLAI GOGOL: THE COMET

Gogol's artistry, concentrated as it was into a period of just eight years (1829–36), has been likened to the lifespan of a comet:

> Bursting suddenly upon the landscape, burning itself out quickly, but transforming the configuration of Russian literary culture.

(Ehre, in Gogol 1980: ix)

With only three plays to his name – *The Marriage*, *The Gamblers* and *The Government Inspector* – Gogol's explosive impact is surprising, particularly as almost all of his reputation as a dramatist rests on the last play in this list. But by the time Meyerhold produced *The Government Inspector*, Gogol was firmly established as a comic genius and his play was inextricably connected to some of the biggest names in Russian theatre history: Mikhail Shchepkin, Konstantin Stanislavsky and Michael Chekhov. After Meyerhold, came other significant productions of the play – including Georgy Tovstonogov's staging in 1972 and, in 1985, Richard Eyre's production for the National Theatre in London. Perhaps the image of Gogol as a comet points not only to his fiery presence at the time but also to his play's enduring ability to 'come round again' and enlighten new audiences.

Gogol was born in the Ukraine in 1809, at a pivotal time in Russian history. Developing later than most European countries, Russia was slowly moving away from its feudal past and waking up to the influence of capitalism. Russia's professional theatre was only fifty years old and the influence of Europe was just beginning to impact on the native culture. In short, it was a time of transition and transition creates tensions, between the customs of the past and the needs of the future. Gogol was at the heart of many of these tensions. His work was acclaimed by left- and right-wing critics alike. He was a figure of radicalism as well as of conservatism. He founded the new movement of Realism but used well-established conventional caricatures to do so. He wrote caustic social satire, but escaped the wrath of the censor.

Indeed, the period in which he was writing was simultaneously a 'golden age' of Russian literature and a period of frightening Tsarist repression. Even though Nicholas I 'turned his country into a barracks staffed by spies and informers' (Worrall 1982: 19), stifling all manner of creative expression, Gogol was part of a burgeoning of home-grown literary talent, including the novelist Dostoevsky and Gogol's friend Pushkin. (A similar tension between State and artist was to be found in the latter part of Meyerhold's career, although in his case the Tsar's oppressive force had been replaced by the equally totalitarian General Secretary of the Communist Party, Joseph Stalin.)

At first, Gogol wanted to be part of the bureaucratic world of nineteenth-century Russia, moving to its capital, St Petersburg, in 1828 and finding work in the Ministry of the Interior. But he quickly tired of the ministry and moved from what he called such 'stupid and senseless work' (Magarshack 1957: 69) to a teaching career, first in an Institute of Young Ladies and then as a history lecturer at the University. After a promising start, his performance as an academic went the same way as his career in the ministry, a result no doubt of his sheer hopelessness as a lecturer! Turgenev, an equally gifted dramatist and friend to Gogol, recognised immediately that his talents lay elsewhere.

> We were all convinced . . . that he had no idea of history, and that . . . professor [Gogol] had nothing in common with Gogol the writer.
>
> (Magarshack 1957: 102)

By the end of 1835 Gogol had accepted Turgenev's argument. He left teaching and dedicated his time exclusively to writing, completing in that year alone an impressive range of work, including his dramatic masterpiece, *The Government Inspector*.

For this play, Gogol's creative energy was at its peak. It took him under two months to write and just four more to get passed by the censor, rehearsed and staged at the Aleksandrinsky Imperial Theatre in St Petersburg. By one of those strange coincidences so often thrown up by history, it was the very same theatre Meyerhold was to work in, over seventy years later during his Dapertutto period.

GOGOL'S *GOVERNMENT INSPECTOR*

WHAT HAPPENS IN THE PLAY

Gogol's play hinges on the trademark convention of comedy – mistaken identity. The dignitaries of an unnamed provincial town, hundreds of miles from anywhere, have become accustomed to their particular way of life. Led by the Mayor, they are vain, self-interested, corrupt and divisive, values which are rewarded in this unfortunate town. But something has arisen to undermine the status quo. The Mayor has received a letter from his friend warning of an impending visit from a Government Inspector – an official charged with rooting out the very practices which have become second nature to the town's ruling class.

ACT 1

Flushed with panic, the Mayor invites his governing council to his house to tell them the news. They are: the Judge, Lyapkin-Tyapkin; the Charities Warden, Zemlyanika; the Schools Superintendent, Khlopov; the Physician, Doctor Gibner; and the Postmaster, Shpyokin. Later they are joined by two landowners, Dobchinsky and Bobchinsky, and by the Chief of Police – all of the town's officials crammed into the Mayor's room.

In any other town the Mayor's news would be highly confidential. But in this provincial backwater the people thrive on whispers, forgotten confidences and shared intelligence. Despite the Mayor's grandiose attempts to capitalise on the moment, the Postmaster has already heard the news and the two landowners, also operating on third-hand information, burst into the meeting with news of a discovery: the Inspector, they claim, has already arrived and is staying at the local inn.

Thus, the seed of delusion is planted in the minds of the officials. Khlestakov, a lowly clerk from St Petersburg, on his way home from the capital, is elevated in the eyes of the town to a senior government official. He may not look the part but that's because he's travelling 'incognito', the people reason. They automatically assume, of course, that the St Petersburg government operates in the same underhand manner as they do.

ACT 2

Thinking fast, the Mayor suggests that he visits Khlestakov in his hotel room to begin a process of covert persuasion or 'buttering up'. First, Khlestakov's bill must be paid, then he must come and stay with the Mayor and after that he must be wined and dined, with an all-expenses-paid tour of the town thrown in. For Khlestakov and his servant Osip, the Mayor's visit to their room comes just in time, saving them from certain eviction at the hands of the landlord for not paying their bills.

ACT 3

We rejoin the town's 'best' after Khlestakov has been taken for the tour. The officials once again crowd into a room in the Mayor's house and Khlestakov is introduced to the family: Anna, the Mayor's wife, and Marya, his daughter. Now decidedly drunk, Khlestakov's natural arrogance and imagination lead him to concoct an elaborate and ever more magnified version of his life in St Petersburg. In an attempt to impress both Anna and Marya, Khlestakov concludes his outburst with the ludicrous claim that he is to be created a field marshal as early as tomorrow. He then makes a hasty exit to sleep it all off! With wanton ambition and deep-seated pretensions to be 'better than they are', the townspeople, including the wily Mayor, swallow all of Khlestakov's lies.

ACT 4

Next day, the Judge and his fellow councillors plan to 'buy the ear' of Khlestakov. One by one they approach the hungover clerk to persuade him to accept a bribe. Always needy and open to offers, Khlestakov accepts each one, raising the stakes as the officials flock through his room. Next in line are the workers, led by a chorus of indignant shopkeepers, eager to inform on the corrupt practices of the Mayor. True to form, Khlestakov soon loses interest and, like a tired child, rejects the remaining petitions. Instead, he composes a letter to his friend, basking in his new-found status and satirising the townspeople. Osip, the thinking half of the duo, has made him aware that their luck is bound to run out soon, so Khlestakov – at this point behaving like a hormonal teenager – attempts to woo the Mayor's wife *and* his daughter. He concludes the act with a perfunctory offer of marriage – to Marya – and then departs swiftly, his pockets stuffed with the Mayor's money.

ACT 5

With a field marshal for a son-in-law, the Mayor revels in his family's fortune, accepting the applause of a host of guests all scrabbling for a piece of their new-found prosperity. That is, until the Postmaster arrives, who, in an echo of the first act, brings in a letter of monumental significance. As a habitual reader of everyone's mail, the Postmaster has opened Khlestakov's letter to his friend. In doing so he is forced to see himself and the rest of his corrupt colleagues through someone else's eyes, a vision he particularly enjoys sharing with the Mayor. The panic that ensues is only heightened by the final revelation: the real Government Inspector has arrived and is awaiting the Mayor's presence at the inn. Each character turns slowly to stone as the cataclysmic response to the news literally petrifies the company. We have arrived back at the grotesque dumb show with which we began this chapter.

I have summarised the story of the play in some detail for two reasons: (1) so that, before you have actually read the play, you have a sound grasp of the events and the order in which they occur – you should then be able to put the theatrical choices made by Meyerhold into some kind of context; and (2) so that you have enough material to go on for the following practical exercise:

Now you have recorded your findings, you will have begun the process of making practical notes on three key areas of theatrical analysis: plot, characterisation, and themes and symbols.

Box 3.1

- Recalling Marinetti's speed-version of *Othello* from the last chapter, get into a group of four (although any size, including solos will do).
- As a group read the plot summary above.
- Tear up some paper into a number of small pieces, about the size of an envelope.
- Start the stopwatch.
- Spend three minutes deciding upon the main events of the play.
- Perform a three-minute version of your edited play, using the pieces of paper as props in as many ways as you can.

Now, reflect on the choices made in the following manner:

- List the events you chose to include in your three-minute version.
- List the characters you included in your three-minute version and note briefly how you distinguished between them.
- List the number of different things you used the paper for.

PLOT (THE ORGANISATION OF EVENTS)

When Gogol sat down to compose *The Government Inspector* he had a story in his head – given to him by Pushkin as a matter of fact. In the process of writing the play, he then had to decide how to *tell* that story. In other words, he translated a chronological narrative into a *plot*. (You have done something similar in creating your three-minute version of Gogol's play, devising a plot from a plot!)

There are some things worth noting about Gogol's plot before we see what Meyerhold chose to do with it:

1   It is divided up into five acts, the traditional subdivision of a full-length play at the time.
2   All of the action takes place within the isolated town.
3   The action is squeezed into a period of less than two days.
4   Act 2 is set in the hotel room. All the other acts are set in the same room in the Mayor's house.
5   Khlestakov is only present in the middle of the play – Acts 2–4.
6   The Mayor appears in every act.

7   The play has a carefully constructed cyclical form: it begins with the announcement of an Inspector (the false one) and ends with the announcement of an Inspector (the real one); it begins with a letter which *conceals* the truth and ends with a letter which *reveals* the truth; it begins in panic, with the Mayor surrounded by his citizens and ends in panic in the same way.

Effectively, Gogol sticks closely to the dramatic unities in *The Government Inspector*, setting the whole piece in the one location (with a switch within the town to the hotel), over a period of little more than twenty-four hours. He concentrates the appearances of his anti-hero (Khlestakov) into the middle of the play, while the Mayor has an overarching and controlling function throughout. The pivotal action of the play is the gradual exposure of Khlestakov to the townspeople, one after another: first, in Act 2, to the Mayor, Dobchinsky and Bobchinsky; next to the Mayor's family, and then, in Act 4, to a whole parade of people, from the Judge to the Sergeant's Widow. Khlestakov is thus revealed as a kind of 'serial responder' to the town's community.

CHARACTERISATION

First, look back to the list of characters gathered around the Mayor in Act 1 – their names give us a clue as to the kind of characters they are. Some of these clues are obvious – Dobchinsky and Bobchinsky are clearly a duet, for example. But some of them are hidden in Gogol's language – Zemlyanika means 'strawberry', for instance, and Khlestakov, 'whippersnapper'. To help us out, Gogol provided detailed notes to some of the characters, in an article entitled 'Advice to Those Who Would Play *The Government Inspector* as it Ought to be Played', published after his death in 1846:

> KHLESTAKOV: Everything about him is surprising, unexpected. For a considerable length of time he cannot even surmise why people are showing him such attention. . . . The actor playing this role must have an extremely multifaceted talent, capable of expressing the diverse characteristics of a person.
>
> MAYOR: He senses that he is a sinner, attends church . . . but the temptation of easy gain is great. From beginning to end he finds himself in a more

> heightened emotional state than he has ever experienced. . . . Shifting
> from terror to hope and joy excites his senses.
>
> ZEMLYANIKA: Physically gross, but a subtle crook. . . . Despite his clumsiness
> and obesity, he is always quick on his toes.
>
> DOB/BOBCHINSKY: Both are short, squat, have little pot-bellies, and resemble
> one another in the extreme . . . the actor must ache with curiosity and be
> afflicted with a wagging tongue if he wants to play these roles well.
>
> KHLOPOV: He quivers like a leaf at the news of the government inspector: all
> [the actor] has to do is convey perpetual terror.
>
> (Gogol 1980: 170–4)

There are several characteristics here which prefigure Meyerhold's style
of acting: the clear delineation of the *external* features of the role, the
sharp changes in characters' emotional states, the sense of Khlestakov
as a 'montage of different masks' (see Chapter 2), and the consistent
feeling of surprise and contradiction in many of the parts.

But, in spite of these features, Gogol also informs us in this essay
that the characters must *not* be caricatured, 'exaggerated or hackneyed'
(ibid.: 169). Instead, the parts must be played modestly and sincerely
with the actor looking to 'common mankind' (ibid.) for a model. With
such heightened expressivity highlighted in his notes for the actors, this
realistic note appears contradictory.

In fact, Gogol's direction is pointing to the serious intention behind
his play. He didn't want it to be written off as a superficial vaudeville,
composed simply as a diversion for the upper classes. He saw *The
Government Inspector* as a didactic piece, designed with an intelligent and
'detached' (ibid.) audience in mind. The play's purpose, he argued,
was to pinpoint the failings of society and then hold them up for
scrutiny, aims which could scarcely be met if the actors resorted to
empty caricature.

Ninety years on, this underlying 'realism', or social message,
appealed in equal measure to Meyerhold, whose own pursuit of a
detached and critical audience was never far away from Gogol's. Indeed
he went as far as to reject some of his trademark influences in the pursuit
of the Gogolian style:

> We must avoid in particular, anything which smacks of buffoonery. We mustn't
> take anything from the *commedia dell'arte*. . . . The course to be held is one
> which leads towards tragedy.
>
> (Worrall 1972: 76)

THEMES AND SYMBOLS

Take a look back at the list of things you symbolised with the paper. They will probably include the Mayor's and Khlestakov's letters – two pivotal props in the play which open and close the piece. Your list may also have included the petitions from the workers, perhaps juxtaposed with the bribes of the Judge and his colleagues. You may have transformed the paper into a love note or a poem to symbolise Khlestakov's wooing of the Mayor's wife and daughter. And, at some point, you almost certainly will have used them as roubles to stuff Khlestakov's pockets.

Using such a simple and transformable material as paper to make different props focuses attention indirectly on some of the underlying images and themes in the play. Think of the associations which come with these props and we get a direct indication of Gogol's thematic content. Such a list could include: officialdom, bureaucracy, corruption, secrecy, oppression, the power of the pen, the power of the rouble, power itself (and its abuses), coercion, manipulation and role play.

Now, if we connect these ideas with some of the other themes in Gogol's play we can begin to get an indication of its complexity. I'll keep the list down to those themes which engaged Meyerhold in his production: the dream, greed versus hunger, the power of the lie, dislocation, masking and disguise, transformations, the grotesque, sexuality, rich versus poor, bribery, Tsarism, formality and crudity, and madness.

It is a diverse and inspiring list of thematic concerns, some of which we have encountered before (masking, the grotesque) and others which are new – the question of 'unreality' or the dream, for example. It is testament to the richness of Meyerhold's vision that his production – four hours long in total – dealt with all of these themes, weaving them together in a performance of such significance that one commentator called it 'The key to all the secrets of his work' (Symons 1971: 149).

Let's turn, then, to unlocking this much lauded production to see for ourselves how Meyerhold realised these ideas on stage.

MEYERHOLD'S *GOVERNMENT INSPECTOR*

DIRECTOR AS AUTHOR

It has become customary to call the outstanding 1926 production of Gogol's play, 'Meyerhold's *Government Inspector*', but before we sweep over this shift of emphasis let's recognise the significance of substituting director for playwright. After all, naming Meyerhold as the 'author' of the production constitutes a massive challenge to the hegemony of the playwright. It is a categorical statement in favour of the 'theatre theatrical' as opposed to the literary theatre and it marks in general terms the ascendancy of the director in the twentieth century.

In the case of Meyerhold, the designation was not just making a philosophical point. It was a practical indication of the extent to which Meyerhold was prepared to adapt Gogol's text to his own ends. During the process of rehearsal and performance Meyerhold changed:

- The structure of the text (from acts to episodes).
- The genre of the text (from comedy to tragicomedy).
- The setting for the play as a whole (from an undefined provincial backwater to the capital).
- Individual locations within the play (from just the hotel and the room in the Mayor's house to multiple locations inside and outside the house).
- The number of characters (specifically introducing three new characters).

In making these changes, he worked not from one canonical text but from all six versions created by Gogol in the drafting and redrafting process. Meyerhold also looked further afield for inspiration, using ideas from Gogol's final play *The Gamblers*, as well as material from his novels and short stories. Although this radical approach to Gogol had its critics (those who thought it was extending the remit of the director too far), Meyerhold's creativity offers us a model of directing/devising today. The underlying principles he espoused in his production are as pertinent now as they ever were:

- Be bold with your vision of the production.
- Research around the text, using as many different and related sources as possible.
- Make connections between the context of the play and conditions today.
- Be prepared to adapt the text to meet the needs or desires of your company.
- Integrate your training into your performance work.

THE PRODUCTION

In order to illustrate how Meyerhold synthesised his ideas into one theatrical vision for his *Government Inspector*, I am going to revisit some of the key theoretical terms encountered in the previous chapter with specific reference to the production. I am also going to anticipate some of the key skills material in Chapter 4 and try to highlight the kind of training underlying the performances in the play. We'll look at the following interconnected areas: montage in practice; musicality and rhythm; the design; acting style; the training beneath; and the grotesque.

MONTAGE IN PRACTICE

Central to Meyerhold's adaptation of Gogol was the reorganising of the text. He rejected the five-act structure detailed above and structured the play in terms of episodes, numbering fifteen in all:

Gogol's *Government Inspector*	Meyerhold's *Government Inspector*
Act 1	Episode 1: Chmykhov's Letter
	Episode 2: An Unforeseen Occurrence
Act 2	Episode 3: After Penza
Not in Gogol	Episode 4: Unicorn
	Episode 5: Filled with the Tend'rest Love
Act 3	Episode 6: The Procession
	Episode 7: Behind a Bottle of 'Tolstobriucha'
Not in Gogol	Episode 8: An Elephant Brought to its Knees
Act 4	Episode 9: Bribes
	Episode 10: Mr High Finance
	Episode 11: Embrace Me Do
	Episode 12: The Blessing
Act 5	Episode 13: Dreams of St Petersburg
	Episode 14: A Fine Old Celebration
	Episode 15: Unprecedented Confusion

(Adapted from Worrall 1972)

This wholesale re-plotting of Gogol's play, and the addition of new scenes, were two clear reasons why Meyerhold declared himself the author of the production. So why make these changes?

First, the shift from acts to episodes changes the *rhythm* of the text. Gogol's five-act structure obeys closely the so-called three Aristotelian unities: time, place and action (although Aristotle actually only mentioned two). Over a period of less than two days, with the vast majority of the time spent in the Mayor's chambers, the action builds gradually to a crescendo (the dumb show). Meyerhold's episodes fragmented this gradual rhythmic development, creating instead a series of shorter 'hits' or shocks. Coupled with his use of multiple locations, the result of this kind of editing was to develop a more fluid and *associative* feel. Norris Houghton contrasts Meyerhold's approach with the seamless arrangement of scenes in Stanislavsky's theatre:

> At the MXAT [Moscow Art Theatre] these *kuski* [bits] are segments of text which are rehearsed separately but when performed flow without a break, so that one is aware only of the *continuity* of the act. Meyerhold divided the act into small episodes so that each ... example of the *jeu de théâtre*, may have *individual* expression. ... Thus the whole production becomes like an 'improvization' or 'variations on a theme'.
>
> (Houghton 1938: 122, my emphases)

It is no surprise, then, that when Stanislavsky staged the play he chose to accentuate the feeling of 'continuity' by telescoping the action of Gogol's drama into one day. (He played the last act in ever-dwindling light as the sun set on the Mayor and his community.) Meyerhold's episodic structuring retained Stanislavsky's principle of segmenting the play into named 'bits', but rejected the idea of overall continuity. Instead, each episode could be viewed *individually*, as a self-supporting 'play in itself', or a '*jeu de théâtre*', as Meyerhold put it – the author's 'thought in theatrical form' (ibid.: 117).

This brings me to the second reason for the episodic treatment: *montage*. Meyerhold's production of *The Government Inspector* conformed to Eisenstein's theory of montage, encountered in the previous chapter. It was structured to maximise the theatrical impact of the play on the audience using short sharp shocks or 'attractions' and it played with the spectators' capacity to link ideas, juxtaposing different images to create another (arguably higher) level of meaning. In short, the episodic structure led Meyerhold to think like a film director, serving up the action in what he called a series of 'close-ups' (Rudnitsky 1981: 390), contrasted with wide-shots. I will return to this point when we talk about the production's design, but here the point concerns the audience: how did they assimilate what was fed to them in these close-ups?

The best way to answer this question is to look at an example: episodes 7–12. At this point in Gogol's play (the end of Act 3), Khlestakov has collapsed from drink and departs for the night. The officials allow him a night to sleep it off and visit him the next day (in Act 4). But Meyerhold saw an opportunity to create some vivid associations in the audience's mind:

Episode	Content of scene	Thematic associations
7	Khlestakov's boasting	Drunkenness/The power of the lie
8	Khlestakov's nightmare vision	Drunkenness/Desire/Corruption
9	The bribe machine	Drunkenness/Bribery/Corruption
10	The merchants' petitions	Injustice/Indifference/Bribery
11	Khlestakov's wooing	Lust/Desire/Bourgeois formality
12	The betrothal	Unreality/Indifference/Corruption

Filling in material not originally included in Gogol's text, Meyerhold moved from the end of the boasting scene (Episode 7) with Khlestakov asleep on the sofa, to Episode 8, 'An Elephant Brought to its Knees'. This latter *jeu de théâtre* saw Khlestakov visited by a nightmarish gallery of townspeople, filing past him as he 'slept' on the sofa. Episode 9, 'Bribes', then merged all the separate inducements offered by the officials into one terrifying theatrical moment, a 'bribe machine' (see Figure 3.2). Simultaneously all the officials' hands appeared from doors at the back, mechanically waving packets of money and chanting. Episode 10 moved to the merchants' petitions. With a huge table slanted across the stage to separate the two parties, the shopkeepers assailed Khlestakov en masse, urging him to support their cause. Episode 11 had Khlestakov dancing a formal quadrille with Marya and Anna, and declaring his undying love for each of them respectively. Finally, Episode 12 staged a trance-like blessing for Khlestakov and Marya before the former abruptly departed leaving the family in a continued state of somnambulism.

Figure 3.2
Meyerhold's *Government Inspector*: 'Bribes', 1926

Following the thread of associations from episode to episode allows us to see the impact of Meyerhold's montage. What, for Gogol, was simply a change of acts, marking the end of one day and the dawning of another, becomes in Meyerhold's version a richly suggestive juxtaposition of ideas. The drunkenness of the previous episode (7) is carried over into the scenes of bribery. The next episode (8) becomes strangely distorted, therefore, by Khlestakov's inebriated perspective. This justifies the nightmarish expressions on the townspeople's faces and their dreamlike status, drawn as they are from Khlestakov's lustful imaginings. As Lunacharsky, the government minister for Arts and Education at the time, describes:

> He dreams of lines of flirting women, of trembling hands with offerings stretched out to him, of piles of envelopes with money falling down on him like rain.
>
> (Lunacharsky 1978: 67)

This image, once implanted in the audience's mind, is then juxtaposed with the bribe machine episode (9), when the officials shower him with money for real. Associations between the images of money, bribery, self-indulgence and drunkenness thus build as we enter into the next three episodes 10–12. The final idea, of course, which is implicit in Gogol but exploded out of Meyerhold's montage, is that Khlestakov's wooing of the women and his ultimate betrothal to Marya is also a corrupt and distorted commercial exchange, albeit of a higher order.

By far the best way to get a feeling for what Meyerhold was doing with his montage is to create an 'episode' of your own. That way you can begin to see how Meyerhold's mind was working when he approached Gogol's text, a definite bonus if you are to take this kind of practice any further. Box 3.2 on the next page gives a suggestion as to how you might begin this process, using Meyerhold's idea of 'filling in' material absent from the text.

MUSICALITY AND RHYTHM

At this point we need to step back and revisit the idea that Meyerhold's episodic structure celebrates the *individuality* of each scene. Clearly, this can only partly be true if what we have said about his use of montage is correct. A montage only begins to have an effect when it is viewed

Box 3.2

- Take Gogol's text (Steven Mulrine's 1997 translation is a relatively new and accessible version) and read Act 1 (pp. 3–18).
- Discuss the major events, focusing mainly on the Mayor's reading of his letter.
- Working individually, recreate, in your imagination, the journey the letter might have taken to get to the Mayor's front door. Remember, the town is in the middle of nowhere and Russia is an immense country. The letter could have passed through many different environments – from snowscapes to sunny beaches.
- Share your thoughts and collate a picture of the most elaborate journey imaginable.
- Split into smaller groups and divide the journey up between you.
- Working primarily in a physical way, restricting the use of voice to ambient noises only, recreate the journey of the letter. The only prop you can use is a piece of paper to symbolise the letter.
- Link the work by insisting that one of the group passes the letter on to the next group. Again, ensure this transition is imaginative and well executed.
- Perform the episode, defining the space by locating a symbolic letterbox somewhere on stage (a chair will do). The episode can then conclude with the delivery of the letter.
- Reflect on the work created and discuss the effect of juxtaposing this episode with the opening of Act 1.

as a whole, when the collision of theatrical images is processed by the brain and an overall response is activated. Stand-alone scenes, then, need an overall structure and for Meyerhold this came from music; he even coined a new term for the integration of music and action in his production of *The Government Inspector*: 'musical realism'.

This much-debated term encapsulates a number of ideas, both large and small. In particular, it has implications for how we understand three key aspects of Meyerhold's theatrical thinking:

1   His overall vision of the actor.
2   His orchestration of action within scenes.
3   His overall approach to the play.

For the most fundamental of these questions, his overall vision of the actor, Paul Schmidt, a translator of writings on Meyerhold, offers a helpful analogy:

> When you watch [the Japanese musician] Yo-Yo Ma play the cello, you watch the physicality of the performance. That is, his physical relationship with the instrument and the way his body moves – that's all you can see, you can't see his mind, his training. You can watch his body move, his features, his face move and you listen to the music as he makes it. Impossible to slip even a knife point between the physicality of what you see and the music itself. You are watching a physical embodiment of the music.
>
> (1998: 83)

As a strings player himself, this explanation would have appealed to Meyerhold. The actor must emulate the integration of music and movement achieved naturally by a great musician. What Yo-Yo Ma is exhibiting is precisely this: an unconscious and seamless synthesis of movement and music, underpinned by years of training. He has achieved the state of 'physical musicality'.

But the actor has more work to do than this. Yo-Yo Ma's movements may be deeply informed by his understanding of the music he is making, but they are nevertheless arbitrary. He's in a constant state of improvisation as far as his external features are concerned. Meyerhold's actors had to *consciously* embody a very precisely prescribed physical score – remember Ilinsky's lifting of the glass from the last chapter – and had little room for any deviations from that score. In a sense the biomechanical actor has to think the other way round – to 'make movement' and imbue it with a sense of musicality. In Meyerhold's own words: 'The actor must know how to act "with the music" and not "to the music"' (Gladkov 1997: 115).

One such actor who understood perfectly this distinction was Erast Garin, Meyerhold's choice for the pivotal role of Khlestakov. Garin's interpretation of the clerk from St Petersburg clearly embodied this concept of musicality. Indeed, the contemporary descriptions of his performance point consistently to his *dance-like* quality, the result, perhaps, of his creative fusion of music and movement.

This was no more evident than in Episode 7, when Khlestakov/Garin danced a drunken reel, staggering from sofa to chair and from wife to daughter, as he told his ever more fanciful autobiography. The entire scene was dictated by the rhythmic shifts of Garin. First, as he began his speech, those gathered were entranced by the slow rhythms of his hypnotic tale, then he leapt up at the sound of Marya shrieking, jerking convulsively and causing the officials to tremble. He then boldly disarmed one of the soldiers and swung his sabre perilously around his head, before collapsing into the Mayor's arms (see Bogdanov 1997, for a fragment of this moment on film). The action was underscored by a waltz entitled 'The Fire of Desire Burns in My Blood', stressing in musical terms one of the overpowering themes of the scene and anticipating Khlestakov's efforts at seduction in Episode 11.

Rudnitsky makes explicit the musicality of Meyerhold's approach in this scene:

> The director's score for the episode was built on the sudden, practically unfounded alteration of Khlestakov's rhythms. Khlestakovianism was revealed by the lack of motivation for the rhythmic shifts and was brought to a concentration of essential tragic absurdity when the officials, trembling with terror, shook and stood helplessly before the snoring monster from St Petersburg.

(Rudnitsky 1981: 402)

Thus, the absurdity of the officials' plight was communicated through the rhythmic structure of the scene. The erratic movements of Garin's Khlestakov somehow symbolised the ludicrous and illogical fawning of the town's dignitaries. Meyerhold's directorial score, his rhythmic orchestration of the activities of his cast, worked to reveal the themes of the episode and to determine its tragicomic genre. It was an essentially *operatic* approach with movement, sound and speech all playing their part in the creation of meaning.

This snapshot from the production gives an idea of Meyerhold's overall intentions. He viewed the actor and the composer in the same terms: both were charged with the task of expressive communication within a tightly controlled time structure. Meyerhold's job was to oversee the process so that the 'variations on a theme', as Houghton called the episodes, came together in a coherent manner.

In a very real way, Meyerhold was a kind of *conductor* of the production, defining a precise structure within which his actors could find their own expression. Ultimately the use of 'real' music, live or recorded, was subordinate in his mind to the actors internalising the *concept* of musicality, as Garin managed to do in the scene above. In fact, Meyerhold wanted finally to drop the use of any musical soundtrack, defining a vision of the performer which is reminiscent of Schmidt's cello player:

> Music is [the actor's] best helper. It doesn't even need to be heard, but it must be felt. I dream of a production rehearsed to music but performed without music. Without it and yet with it, because the rhythm of the production will be organized according to music's laws and each performer will carry it within himself.
>
> (Gladkov 1997: 115)

DESIGN

The keystone in realising this musical vision of the play was the production's design. Meyerhold believed this so firmly that he took responsibility for it himself, recognising that his complex orchestration of events could only successfully be achieved if the design was fully in harmony with the rest of the production. There *was* a credited designer for the show, Victor Kiselyov, but he simply delivered Meyerhold's overall concept.

The design is a crucial aspect of any production, primarily because it organises the key dimension of an actor's world: *space*. As such, a design dictates:

- the movements of individual performers;
- the physical relationship *between* characters;
- the composition of any groupings or sub-groupings;
- the atmosphere of a particular scene.

A design also encompasses the look and feel of the props and furniture: those objects most closely related to the work of the actor. It can create a visual context for the action of the play and may suggest important details such as period, place and social position.

Rejecting Gogol's provincial location, Meyerhold set his *Government Inspector* in a city just like the capital, St Petersburg. He retained the Tsarist context of the play and used the production to satirise pre-revolutionary bourgeois values. Many critics, though, saw the parallels with *post*-revolutionary officialdom, and these cannot have been entirely unwarranted. To emphasise the extravagance of the ruling class, Meyerhold portrayed the Mayor's house as vast, setting each episode in a different room and giving the women, in particular, added costume changes. He also exaggerated the size of the Mayor's furniture, creating a distorted and unsettling vision of a moneyed class.

But perhaps most important of all the design choices made by Meyerhold was the way in which he chose to 'serve up' his production to his spectators. He understood that it was not so much *what* they viewed but *how* they viewed the production that was important. The 'rhythm' of the episodic structure had in some way to be translated into the design so that the audience could appreciate the play in its new format. Meyerhold's answer was bold and ingenious, he called it 'kinetic staging'.

The word 'kinetic' comes from the ancient Greek verb *kinein*, 'to move', and Meyerhold's design was founded on this principle. It was a 'moving' stage. He realised that unless the scenery could be turned around between scenes very quickly the whole production would come to a standstill. So, in characteristic fashion, Meyerhold looked back into the past to find a solution for the present. He created a modern-day classical stage, fusing the *theatron* of the ancient Greeks with the up-to-date cinema techniques of the day.

The backdrop was dominated by a series of eleven doors, fashioned out of hardwood and arching across the whole of the back of the stage. Two more pairs of doors were situated on each side, towards the forestage, totalling fifteen – the number of episodes in the play. This was the 'wide-shot' or open stage, used for five of the episodes. The rest of the scenes (with one exception) were staged on a tiny platform, just 4.25 by 3.5 metres (Braun 1995: 231), which was wheeled out silently through the middle doors at the back. Here was the similarity with the Greek stage, for Meyerhold's truck closely resembled the *ekkyklema* of classical tragedy, designed to roll out precisely composed tableaux of death in plays such as Aeschylus's *Oresteia*. Meyerhold also used his *ekkyklema* to reveal frozen figures, but with his 'close-ups' the ensemble sprung into life as the episode began. The only other scene – Episode 3 – was flown in as an entirely separate set.

The detailed pattern of wide-shots (on the open stage) and close-ups (on the platform) was as follows:

Episode	Title	Staging
1	Chmykhov's Letter	Platform
2	An Unforeseen Occurrence	Platform
3	After Penza	Flown-in 'room'
4	Unicorn	Platform
5	Filled with the Tend'rest Love	Platform
6	The Procession	Open stage (+ balustrade)
7	Behind a Bottle of 'Tolstobriucha'	Platform (+ split balustrade)
8	An Elephant Brought to its Knees	Open stage
9	Bribes	Open stage
10	Mr High Finance	Open stage (+ long table)
11	Embrace Me Do	Platform
12	The Blessing	Platform
13	Dreams of St Petersburg	Platform
14	A Fine Old Celebration	Platform
15	Unprecedented Confusion	Open stage

This table of Meyerhold's staging reveals some interesting facts about his directorial thinking for *The Government Inspector*:

1 The uniqueness of the scene in the hotel room – After Penza.
2 The concentration of attention on the small platform, even for large scenes.
3 The range of different locations suggested by the platform.
4 The extent to which he felt it necessary to delineate the space of the open stage with other pieces of furniture or scenery.
5 The constant need to keep the production *moving*.

In terms of the staging of After Penza, Meyerhold was honouring Gogol's original text. The hotel *is* unique in the play. It contains the only scene to take place outside of the Mayor's house, the only moment where we see *real* poverty and grime as opposed to the metaphorical dirt of corruption. Flying the whole episode in from above stressed that the hotel was 'another world', populated not by masters, as with the rest of the play, but by servants.

The second point relates to one of the boldest design choices of all. With a large stage and a huge cast at his disposal, Meyerhold chose to restrict the majority of the action to a platform a little less than fifteen metres square. This did not mean, however, that he neglected to use the full ensemble for the platform scenes. On the contrary, Meyerhold meticulously composed huge canvases made up of fifty or more actors, all beautifully crammed on to the platform. He likened it to 'construct[ing] a palace on the tip of a needle' and it was a central part of his philosophy of acting. 'Having constructed such a platform, it became possible for me to comprehend the beauty of . . . *self-limitation*,' he argued, adding that *restrictions* encourage 'true craftsmanship' (Rudnitsky 1981: 391). It was a message which spoke volumes, not just about the production but about the acting system which informed the work: biomechanics.

The last three points may be dealt with as one. The use of the platform allowed the multiple locations of the production to be changed almost instantaneously, for there was not just one platform but two. While one scene was playing in front of the doors the next scene could be set behind them, and at the end of the episode the two could be swapped. Thus, the production was always 'on the move', fluidly transforming from location to location and punctuated by the open-stage scenes. These Meyerhold used carefully, either to allow for an unusually expansive vista (as in the Bribes scene), to suggest the outdoors (as in The Procession) or to accentuate the divide between Khlestakov and the townspeople (as in Mr High Finance). Meyerhold also reserved the open stage for the final episode, stripping back all the properties and furniture used before to present his gallery of mannequins: the emptiness of Tsarist Russia underlined in a deft theatrical coup.

ACTING STYLE: CHAPLIN MEETS HOFFMANN

If Meyerhold likened his design to the cinema, he also appealed to the movies in describing the style of acting he was looking for in his cast:

> Remember Chaplin . . . what complicated scenes he does, or Keaton – and he acts in a space of a couple of yards, sometimes half that, sometimes simply sitting on a chair.
>
> (Hoover 1974: 160)

Chaplin and Keaton, as silent-movie stars, encapsulated the physical clarity and economy of craft Meyerhold was seeking in his production. Both could express a virtuosic range of skills and yet still hit their mark for the camera. They understood the power of 'composition' on the big screen, using all of their physical resources to tell the story. And they caught the essence of the genre Meyerhold wanted – the mix of tragedy and comedy, melodrama and farce. Meyerhold also recreated the frantic rhythms and knockabout action of the Keystone Cops in the final episode (15), choreographing a comical and panic-stricken exit by the police, following the announcement of the real Inspector's arrival. He enjoyed the satirical mix of authority and buffoonery just as much as the early American film-makers.

The other frequently cited influence is that of E.T.A. Hoffmann (see Chapter 2), especially in relation to Garin's playing of Khlestakov. This is how his first entrance, in After Penza, was described by one critic:

> He appears onstage, a character from some tale by Hoffmann, slender, clad in black with a stiff mannered gait, strange spectacles, a sinister old fashioned tall hat, a rug and a cane, apparently tormented by some private vision.
>
> (Braun 1991: 213)

Hoffmann's influence explained Meyerhold's sinister reading of Khlestakov, also partly inspired by Michael Chekhov's dark portrayal of the character in 1921. The entrance seems consciously to reverse that of Coppelius in Hoffmann's *The Sandman* (1816), who, rather than descending the staircase like Garin, climbs the stairs, putting the fear of God into the child, Nathaniel:

> The image of the cruel sandman now assumed hideous detail within me, and when I heard the sound of clumping coming up the stairs in the evening I trembled with fear and terror.
>
> (Hoffmann 1982: 87)

Meyerhold wanted to induce echoes of this response in his audience, justifying the panicked reactions of the dignitaries in the previous episode by showing Khlestakov as an altogether more calculating and mysterious individual than was customary.

Many critics have highlighted this departure from the tradition of playing Khlestakov, using it as evidence of yet more radical reinterpreting by the director. But Meyerhold's choices were surprisingly in tune with Gogol's view of the character. Although he clearly believed the servant, Osip, to be Khlestakov's mental superior, Gogol does describe the St Petersburg official as 'phantasmagorical', adding, as we noted in the section on characterisation: 'everything about him is surprising, unexpected' (Gogol 1980: 173).

It was this idea of 'unpredictability' that became the leitmotif for the characterisation of Khlestakov: physically, vocally and rhythmically. Like a storyteller, he transformed from one character to another, changing his 'mask', as the critic Boris Alpers noted, to fit the moment. One minute he was an invalid with the Mayor, broken by poverty and clutching a stick, the next he was a puffed-up and accusatory officer, transforming himself with a simple waft of his cloak. Such instability of character served only to increase his air of mystery.

So what was the result of this mixture of Hollywood and Hoffmann? Nick Worrall picks up the account where we left off. Dressed in the black garb described above, Garin paused on the landing of the flown-in scene. Next:

> He came down the stairs. Then, instead of turning into the room, [he] advanced straight forwards, as if threatening to enter the auditorium. Then he stopped, turned suddenly to the left, presenting his profile to the audience and, with a swift movement, cracked his cane sharply across the table. He then detached a [bread] roll [from his button hole] and held it out to Osip – 'Here, it's for you'.
>
> (Worrall 1972: 82)

The fusion of the sinister and the farcical is beautifully caught in this extract. First, like a grim reaper, Khlestakov glides into the space, wielding his cane like a scythe. Next, he plucks an incongruous bread roll from his costume and with great seriousness proffers it to his hungry servant. The moment is both comic and tragic, a collision of ideas perhaps best symbolised in the emblem of the cane: is it Chaplin's or Coppelius's? Take your pick!

THE TRAINING BENEATH: BIOMECHANICS IN *THE GOVERNMENT INSPECTOR*

If you were to compare *The Government Inspector* (1926) with a production from earlier in the decade – *The Magnanimous Cuckold* (1922), for example – you might well conclude that there was *no* evidence of any biomechanics in Meyerhold's masterpiece. Whereas the constructivist stage for Crommelynck's play reflected the new machine age, with the actors recreating the étude of 'The Slap' within the performance, the nineteenth-century setting for *The Government Inspector* seemed far removed from its contemporary context and the performers offered no obvious indications of any biomechanical training.

But this did not mean, of course, that there *was* no training. In fact, Meyerhold's approach to Gogol's play confirmed a new maturity in the way he integrated his teaching in the studio with his directing in the theatre. Rather like his ultimate dream of a musical production without the music, biomechanics was also 'silent' or unseen in *The Government Inspector*. But it was no less influential for that.

Indeed, Meyerhold's seamless assimilation of training and text offers us a model of how to relate 'process' to 'product'. You will quickly find when you begin the exercises in the next chapter that the shapes and rhythms of the études cannot simply be lifted, unchanged, on to a stage and imposed on a character. They must be absorbed, embodied, made part of you in some way. Only then is it possible to exploit creatively the underlying theatrical skills developed by the training. As Meyerhold himself said, 'technique arms the imagination' (Schmidt 1996: 41), and he drew on both to realise his vision of Gogol's drama.

With a trained eye, the 'unseen' elements of biomechanics come into focus. They are evident in the:

- rhythms of the actors;
- discipline of the ensemble;
- constant surprises;
- gestural patterns of the performers;
- dance-like quality of the action;
- extensive 'play with props';
- conscious attention to external form;
- responsiveness of the actors.

Some of these things may not be clear until you read the next chapter, but a good number of these ideas should now be familiar to you. You may indeed be able to add to this list. With these aspects in mind, then, read the following description from one of the most celebrated ensemble moments in the production (Episode 14). See if you can identify the latent influence of biomechanics:

> The small platform was framed by the splendid restless drawing of a gold triple mirror, filled to the limit by figures of officials and their wives, and soldiers. Uniforms shone, women's bare shoulders gleamed. Guests continued to arrive with a happy roar. There was nowhere to sit, chairs were being brought in, floated over heads, rocked, were put down. The Jewish orchestra behind the scenes played a march. . . . The mass of humanity . . . wavered, shifted, babbled and pressed toward the Mayor and Anna Andreevna, who were in the right corner of the platform. Then the postmaster appeared and made his way through the crowd, jumping on chairs, falling down and disappearing from view. When he stopped, finally, clutching the fateful opened letter in his hand, the entire crowd immediately changed its orientation and pressed to the left corner, where the reading began.
>
> (Rudnitsky 1981: 417)

Thus, the moment where the Postmaster reads Khlestakov's incriminating letter is set up. It was a scene which simply could not have been either conceived or achieved without an understanding of biomechanics.

The overall structure of the moment mirrors that of an étude: the *otkaz*, or preparation, is extensive and drawn out as the Postmaster fights to get a seat; the *posil'*, or action, is marked by the ensemble's rapid change of orientation; and the *tochka*, or 'end point', is the instant held by the Postmaster as he prepares to read the letter. (This is the moment which is documented in the famous photograph – see Figure 3.3.)

The rigid discipline of the ensemble testifies to the collective training of biomechanics, slowly building up an unspoken understanding between actors which is underpinned by a strong sense of rhythm. Here, there are two rhythms at work – the individual bumbling of the Postmaster, set against the collective rhythm of the mass as they respond to the new focus and pan round to take in the letter.

The game with the chairs (so reminiscent of the work of Complicite today) is a development from the work with sticks detailed in the next chapter. Props became beautiful in the hands of Meyerhold's actors – a result of arduous work balancing, throwing and catching various objects in the studio. The music of the orchestra lends the whole passage with the chairs a feeling of a formal dance, even though chaos reigns on the platform.

But of course, the final measure of the discipline of this scene is that chaos *doesn't* actually reign. We only see the external and carefully composed *form* of chaos. No one falls off from the huge pyramid, no

Figure 3.3
Meyerhold's
*Government
Inspector:*
'Reading the
letter', 1926

one breaks the rhythmic cohesion of the ensemble, everyone works together to build their palace on a needle point. This must have been the ultimate test of Meyerhold's adage that limitations breed artistry and it can only have come from the training which preaches the same message: biomechanics.

THE GROTESQUE – THE SYNTHESIS OF MEYERHOLD'S IDEAS

By now, is should be clear why Meyerhold's *Government Inspector* is so important. It constitutes the grand synthesis of his ideas. It is empirical evidence of the mature director-author displaying his undisputed talent for directing. I am by no means the first to argue this, but I hope that this chapter has illustrated something new: the way in which this seminal production acted as a locus for so many of Meyerhold's activities and theories.

One of the clearest indicators of this is the extent to which the production achieved Meyerhold's defining style: the grotesque. For the grotesque by nature is synthetic, it borrows from a range of sources and combines them in unusual and thought-provoking ways. It does this with the aim of shifting an audience's perspective, surprising them into new discoveries. For Meyerhold the grotesque was an intrinsic aspect of Gogol's dramaturgy:

> Gogol was fond of saying that funny things often become sad if you look enough at them. This transformation of mirth into sadness is the conjuring trick of Gogol's dramatic style.

(Braun 1991: 211)

Having seen too many frothy, vaudeville-inspired versions of Gogol's text, Meyerhold wanted to shift its genre into the darker, more challenging arena of tragicomedy. He looked to Hoffmann, as we have seen, for one model of the grotesque and to Chaplin for another. He combined slapstick clowning with the stark images of death in the dumb show. He designed his stage so that it could constantly mutate and transform. He peppered the production with theatrical surprises and unexpected delights. He drew out the hitherto understated satirical bite of Gogol's play. He included elements of the mysterious and of 'other worldliness', particularly in the drunken episodes. And, in his creative montage, he 'stretched' the play, reconfiguring it in order to shift the audience's perspective. In a way, this was a theatrical response to what Gogol is saying above about perception: look long enough at this play (just over four hours, in fact) and you will begin to see it differently.

All of these techniques are part of Meyerhold's overarching pursuit of the grotesque. But the ultimate question remains: how did they impact on the audience? The eyewitness testimonies are sharply divided on this question. *The Government Inspector* led to huge debates and disputes in the press and had stimulated three book-long critiques within a year of its opening. This was, of course, the ideal response for Meyerhold, who revelled in controversy and worried if too many people praised his productions.

Such disagreement is in itself evidence of the grotesque at work, challenging its audiences, unsettling them and forcing them to see things differently. Harold Clurman, the American writer and director, who saw the production in the 1920s, puts his finger on this effect beautifully:

> A strange feeling comes from this production: it is very funny and it's very tomblike. It has a definite macabre quality — cold, beautiful, grimacing, distorted and graceful. ... The production ends with the actors running off stage laughing while on stage we see the prototypes who are puppets. Meyerhold's *Revisor* [*The Government Inspector*] is a masterpiece, but somehow not a warming one, it leaves one slightly uncomfortable.
>
> (Clurman 1998: 80)

There could be no better measure of the power of the grotesque, no clearer indication of how seriously Meyerhold had taken Gogol's challenge and how effectively he had risen to it.

There were fewer landmark productions after *The Government Inspector* at the Meyerhold Theatre. Soon the pressure of censorship was to increase to a level which clearly stifled the creativity of the Master. But this time the limitations imposed on Meyerhold were not the kind which led to greater artistry. They led instead to public criticism, to interrogation, to prison and finally to execution. After symbolising such a creative fusion of Meyerholdian techniques, *The Government Inspector* became one of the productions cited as evidence of Meyerhold's anti-governmental stance. It was simply (and chillingly) labelled a 'mistake'.

Vsevolod Meyerhold paid the ultimate price for making things uncomfortable.

4

PRACTICAL EXERCISES

PRACTICE: THE LIVING LINK WITH MEYERHOLD

Imagine a large room, lit from a wall of windows, scruffy but not untidy, perhaps with a ballet bar around the sides. Then think of twenty or more actors within that space, clothed in overalls or working clothes, frozen in a gesture of running. The lines created by the actors' arms and legs are echoed down the studio. Everyone is making the same shape. There is a sense of anticipation.

Abruptly, a voice shouts 'hup' and the actors set off on the run, their arms chopping the air in a bizarre, stylised way. Another shout of 'hup' and the ensemble of actors jump, taking off from the left foot and landing on their right. They are now looking over their shoulders and down to the floor. Once again their figures mirror each other across the room. The effect is like surveying a waxworks museum of sporting stars.

It's 1922 and the actors you are creating in your mind's eye are performing the first actions from what Meyerhold called 'Throwing the Stone' – an étude or physical study, designed to develop and test an actor's basic skills. The studio is in Moscow and the overalled performers are actors in the Meyerhold theatre, training to be part of one of the director's famous ensembles.

Now think again. Imagine that it is not Moscow outside the workshop windows, but somewhere nearer to home. Suppose that it is not 1922 but 2003 and the actors at work are not in Meyerhold's troupe but part of a contemporary training programme in biomechanics somewhere in the UK. How different would this training be? The surprising response to that question is 'not much'! In fact, the physical shape of the étude 'Throwing the Stone' has changed very little in four generations. Our two sessions might be separated by eighty years and by very different cultural conditions, but the practice of biomechanics has been remarkably constant in this time. Why? Because Meyerhold's craft is captured in the body of the actor, preserved in the muscles and bones of performers from the 1920s to today, and passed down from practitioner to practitioner. Only when you begin to explore his work in practice can you gain direct access to this living link with the past.

This chapter is designed to give you the tools to do precisely this. It is written assuming that you will be engaged in a developmental process of training – there is no point doing a one-off, two-hour workshop in biomechanics – and that ultimately you may be planning to lead a workshop with your peers. But you can, of course, read this chapter as someone who wants simply to participate or for a practical elucidation of the theoretical principles encountered earlier. Either way, you will soon find that engaging practically with the ideas in this section will help shed light on many of the other ideas already discussed. Meyerhold may have loved to associate his work with complex theories but the ultimate test of those ideas is in the laboratory, the name he used for the actor's practical studio.

SO WHAT *ARE* THE BASIC SKILLS OF A BIOMECHANICAL ACTOR?

Let's begin with what we might want to gain from a training in Meyerhold's system of acting. Why might twenty actors mimic the externals of an Olympic runner in a dilapidated studio in Moscow? Primarily, to acquire *skills*, skills which are fundamental to the craft of acting: precision, balance, coordination, efficiency, rhythm, expressiveness, responsiveness, playfulness and discipline. You might want to spend a moment thinking about how developed *your* skills are in these areas before reading on.

These skills are interdependent, they support one another and, although we can discuss them in isolation, separating them out in practice is far more difficult. Everything we talk about here will in some way be related to these skills – they underpin the work in biomechanics and, although it takes a considerable time to develop them to a professional standard, it's surprising how quickly you can make progress. Let's deal with them in general terms before we go any further.

PRECISION

Think of anything you have done recently on stage (a gesture, a turn of phrase, an expression) and ask yourself the question: could I do that again? If your honest answer is 'yes, exactly', then you have been acting with a definite sense of precision. But it is more likely to be 'almost'. In some cases it may well be 'do what again?' Try it and see and then think about how close you are to your original performance. Now reflect upon what other skills you need to have in order to recreate a gesture precisely: coordination, balance, discipline and, very probably, an understanding of rhythm. As I said, the skills are all interlinked.

Meyerhold's theatre was based upon a developed level of precision. He looked to the practice of circus performers and acrobats, who depend for their own safety on their ability to repeat precisely a movement or gesture, and he tried to bring the same skills into the theatre. If there is physical risk involved in the work the need for precision is multiplied, but even in the safe environment of a discussion over the dinner table the actor needs to be sure of what he is doing. Meyerhold understood this and understood too that, once a level of precision is brought to bear on any action, the action itself becomes more watchable for an audience.

BALANCE

In normal life the body has an automatic balancing facility, centred in the inner ear. But Meyerhold's theatre called for extraordinary skills of balance. His training reflects this by forcing the actor to *think* about the body's natural capacity to keep balanced. He does this by making things *un*natural, by insisting your feet are parallel when you want them to be at ninety degrees, or by asking you to balance other things – sticks, chairs, even other performers. A balanced actor is a confident actor and a confident actor is someone who wants to share their talents with the audience. Again, the connection is with the circus or with gymnastics, the kinds of performance which create a feeling of pleasure stimulated by being witness to the most remarkable feats. Actors don't have to perform somersaults to achieve this feeling of pleasure. Simply holding the stage with a bold and explicit gesture can evoke the same sensation. As long as you don't wobble!

COORDINATION

From both a personal and a group perspective, coordination is a central skill in performance. Personally, the need to master your own individual moving parts and to exhibit overall control of these parts is essential. This may mean something simple like moving your arms in time with your legs. Or it might mean rather complex levels of coordination where, for example, one part of your body is operating at a different tempo to another, or when one action (tapping your head) is in conflict with another (rubbing your stomach). From a group perspective your individual movements need to operate in harmony with the rest of the ensemble – you need to coordinate your work with the movements and actions of the rest of the cast and with the demands of the particular space.

It's no coincidence, that in looking for a metaphor to describe the term coordination, I've had to use musical and mechanical terms – 'harmony', 'operating', 'moving parts'. Meyerhold's theatre was influenced by both disciplines (the word *biomechanics* itself is a clue to this) and it is worth keeping this in mind as we approach the exercises.

EFFICIENCY

Never waste energy on stage. It's tiring for you and it's uncomfortable for an audience. You need all your physical resources at your command when you are performing in a production in Meyerhold's style and needless gestures or over-elaborate actions simply use up those resources unnecessarily. A novice in middle- or long-distance running understands this immediately, but an untrained actor may spend many months exhausting himself before he realises this fact. For Meyerhold, the model for an actor was a factory worker, forced by the repetitive demands of his work to rationalise the working process and eliminate anything superfluous. If you have ever worked on a production line you'll know how quickly you have to adapt your naturally wasteful actions to the tempo of the machine. You might also know, when you *do* master the demands of the machine and you begin to work efficiently, how visually striking your movements become. They are instinctively fluid, rhythmic and precise.

RHYTHM

Rhythm is one of those mysterious terms in theatre, rather like the word 'movement' in the mouths of football pundits – everyone seems to use it but few would be prepared to explain it! For Meyerhold, rhythm is the glue which binds all the other skills of the actor together. He wasn't in any way mysterious about it. As discussed on p. 55, he broke everything down (from the tiniest gesture to the overall structure of a play) into a tripartite rhythm – a rhythm made up of three parts. He then gave each part a name: *otkaz*, or 'preparation'; *posil'*, or 'action'; and *tochka*, or 'end point'. These three parts are the very building blocks of biomechanical theatre. From the work of an individual actor to the orchestration of large ensembles, from a line in a small scene to the formal analysis of the whole play, *otkaz*, *posil'* and *tochka* determine everything.

EXPRESSIVENESS

Expression is the means by which an actor communicates with an audience. A director gives you a task and it is your job to express this vision to the spectators. There are as many different kinds of expression as there are theatre styles, perhaps as many as there are directors, or even actors. But certain characteristics can easily be highlighted when we are talking about Meyerhold's theatre. Meyerhold's mode of expression was exaggerated, elongated and stylised. He wanted to build stage pictures which expressed the central idea of the scene without the need for words, and he wanted his actors to have the wherewithal to do this. Thus, the actor in Meyerhold's troupe had to be physically fit, agile and flexible, just as the actors of *commedia dell'arte* were in a previous era.

When a biomechanical actor walks on stage there is always some kind of *reaction* from his fellow performers. They may start, do a double-take or rearrange their perspective to compensate for the new arrival. Think of the work of the great silent screen actors (Charlie Chaplin, Buster Keaton, Harold Lloyd) for a model of this kind of expression. They all use a bold, physical style with clear and precise gestures and they all exhibit a beguiling sense of mischief.

RESPONSIVENESS

Of course, if reactions on stage are so important, it follows that, as an actor, you need to be permanently 'switched on', or responsive, to what is happening before you. Have you ever missed a cue on stage because your thoughts were elsewhere? Or found yourself out of step with the rest of the cast because someone else has done something differently? If so, then you will know what the dangers of being *un*-responsive are.

But although all stage actors, by definition, must be able to respond to the unpredictabilities of the live event, Meyerhold's emphasis on the responsiveness of the actor was extreme. His ideal is a kind of 'reflexive' actor, reacting almost instantaneously to a given stimulus, as if shocked by an electric charge. The 'charge' may be any number of things: a sound effect, another line, or an entrance or exit. But whatever it is the response time for the actor must be immediate.

PLAYFULNESS AND DISCIPLINE

I have put these last two skills together as they are two sides of the same coin, in a delicate balance with one another. Too much playfulness and a performance can become self-indulgent and without focus; too little and the spark of creativity which is necessary for any kind of work in the theatre can never catch light. An overly disciplinarian atmosphere in workshops can have this effect, extinguishing the lightness of touch which comes from simple play.

The contemporary accounts of Meyerhold in the rehearsal room highlight both aspects of his character. He was an exacting taskmaster who had a precise vision of what he wanted to see on stage. But although this led him to take a sometimes very authoritative approach in his rehearsals, this atmosphere of control would be punctuated by moments of frolicsome play.

Whether you are participant or leader in a biomechanical workshop it is worth reflecting on this relationship. As a leader you must define the right atmosphere for concentrated and sometimes gruelling physical work. But at the same time you have to be responsive to unforeseen occurrences and be adaptable enough to transform the atmosphere with a different exercise or a change of tack. As a participant you must commit yourself to what are very prescriptive exercises at times. But you must also learn to inject your own individuality into these exercises, to *play* within tightly controlled conditions.

THE EXERCISES

Having defined the underlying principles of biomechanical work, it is now possible to outline the details of some of the practice. Inevitably this is not an all-inclusive checklist of exercises. Work in biomechanics takes years to perfect and the range of sources (from *commedia*, to circus, from Japanese theatre to the Elizabethan stage) does not lend itself to written documentation. But it is possible to put down in writing some introductory work and to characterise the kind of activities which are appropriate to a training in Meyerhold's style of theatre. There are several sources now available in English which give further details of the practice and you are asked to read what follows in conjunction with these, especially the video archives of Aleksei Levinski (1995) and Gennadi Bogdanov (1997, 1998).

There is no strict order to these exercises, but I have organised them to suggest a progressive pattern of work – from general *skills-based exercises*, including a detailed look at the étude 'The Slap' and a revision of basic skills, to those which involve some level of *improvisation*, and finally to work based on *text*. Depending on the intended outcomes of the work you may emphasise different aspects of the practice, choosing specific exercises. This is fine but it is advisable to retain an element of the skills-based work throughout the process so that a proficiency in the key skills indicated in the last section can grow.

First, though, you will need to obtain some basic equipment and undertake some warm-up exercises.

WHAT YOU WILL NEED

You won't need all of the following for each session and, depending on the particular focus of the work, may not need some of them at all. But at some stage the exercises will make use of everything from this list:

- A large room, preferably heated, with a floor which will not perish if you drop things on it.
- A number of metre-length sticks – broom sticks will do but they need to be quite strong. If they are over one metre cut them down – the length of the stick is important.
- A bag of tennis balls – enough for each participant to have one. The same goes for the sticks.
- A sound system.
- A video player.
- A means of documenting the work at times – a video or stills camera.

WARMING UP

Before you begin anything you must warm yourself up. Biomechanics puts all of your muscles under considerable strain and if these muscles are not properly stretched out and warmed up you will injure yourself. There are many ways to do this, either as a group or individually, but however you choose to do it you must make sure that you are physically prepared for the work.

One efficient way to warm up is to work upwards, from your feet to your upper body, neck and head. Begin with flexing the ankles, the calves and the thigh muscles. Once the legs are feeling warmer and more flexible, you can begin to run or walk in different directions. Pause to rotate the hips, to push them forward and back, left and right. Develop a walk which uses an exaggerated movement of the hips and take it across the circle.

Work now on the knees. Sit in a half squat with a straight back. Take the squat lower and lower before straightening the legs to stand again. As a group, with the leader dictating the pace, lower yourself to a kneel without a sound. Stand again, without using your hands to help you up and repeat this cycle. Practise a Cossack dance: the group can even improvise a Russian soundtrack for it!

Move to focusing on the upper body. Isolate the chest and shift it from side to side (left and right) without moving the hips or the stomach. Keep the shoulders parallel to the floor. Try and push the chest forward to make it convex, then back to make it concave. Then, add in the left and right movements so that you can move all the upper chest in a circle – forward, left, back, right – while the lower torso remains stationary. Once again this flexing of the body might express itself in a stylised walk. Put the hips-walk together with the chest movements and begin to see what kind of strange person emerges as you explore the space!

Now pay attention to the head and neck: first, by simply flexing the head in the direction of the four poles – north, east, south and west; then, by improvising different responses using only the movement of the head and neck. These may include 'surprise', 'disgust', 'curiosity', 'panic' or 'lechery'. You can do this in pairs with one partner entering and making an offer and the other partner responding with a counter-offer. Analyse which responses have a forward impetus and which take the head back.

You will find that once this kind of improvisation is set up you will already be using facial expressions to augment the work. So now develop these by thinking of the face as a mask. Warm up the face by making big faces, wide faces, diagonal faces or tiny faces. Again, toss in some suggestions for expressions and try to capture them in a frozen facial expression or mask: 'lust, 'anger', 'shock' and 'hilarity' will all stretch the face in different directions and begin to establish the sense of an external, non-psychological theatre.

There are no definitive guidelines as to how long a warm-up should be, but you want to be happy that all the major muscle groups have been stretched out. A warm-up must also set the right tone. It's like an introduction to an essay – leading us into the work and giving the participants the right tools to understand the following exercises. Think about how you are covering the essential biomechanical skills, even when you are planning the warm-up. In the examples above, the straight warm-up exercises are interspersed with small improvisations and with very early character work. Using this approach, the participants gain a sense of style as well as simply flexing their muscles.

SKILLS-BASED EXERCISES

These include tap steps; work with sticks (with practice in *otkaz*, *posil'* and *tochka*); further work with sticks; work with balls; and études. Let's examine each of these exercises in turn.

TAP STEPS

The basic skills developed here are precision, balance, coordination, rhythm and discipline.

To do tap you must be light on your feet, nimble and able to shift your weight from left to right and from front to back effortlessly. You have to be able to coordinate the top half of your body with the lower half and to perform each precise gesture with a celebratory sense of fun. Above all, you have to have *rhythm* and a desire to share your skill with the audience. The hours of gruelling and mechanical exercises are concealed in the performance of a tap routine as the fluency of the dance form takes over. In that sense it is a good analogy for the training a biomechanical actor undergoes. As the actor moves towards performance, the mechanical repetition of an exercise gives way to a flowing feeling of ease.

If someone in your group has tap experience (and they often do!), grab them and get them to lead some introductory exercises. If not, then you can establish some simple tap movements which will begin to test the basic skills of biomechanics.

Exercise 4.1

Work in a circle:

➤   Divide your foot into two: toe and heel.
➤   Tap out a four/four rhythm – on the right (toe, heel) for two, and then the left (toe, heel) for two.
➤   Using this step move round in a circle, first clockwise then anti-clockwise.
➤   Make sure everyone is keeping to the same overall tempo.
➤   Keeping the four/four step, move towards the centre of the circle so that you are in a tighter arrangement. Move out again.
➤   Using this step, move round in a circle again. You can begin to let your following leg go behind your leading leg so that they cross.

➤ Then alternate the step with the following leg, first behind as before, then in front of your leading leg. You will find yourself naturally leaning into the circle when your leg is in front and out when it is behind. Your upper body will twist from side to side as your following leg weaves in and out of the circle.

➤ Repeat, going round the circle in the other direction.

Once you have the basis for an ensemble-led opening 'dance', it can become more elaborate over a period of weeks.

For example, try a different pattern with your feet – toe (left), heel (right), toe (left), heel (left); then change sides – toe (right), heel (left), toe (right), heel (right). It's difficult at first but slowly you learn to 'forget' what your feet are doing. You can then take this step in all directions.

Next, facing into the circle, return to the basic four/four rhythm and add in your arms – as the left foot is working let the right arm come forward and vice versa. Extend this gesture towards the centre of the circle. On the call of 'hup', freeze. Check your balance and ensure your freeze is held perfectly. On the next call of 'hup' begin again.

Finally, from a neutral position try jumping so that all your weight is on one leg and then shifting this weight to the other leg. Do this shifting skip to a particular rhythm, either set by some music or by the leader counting. Complement the movement of your feet with balancing gestures with your arms. Take the gestures round the circle as a canon. Try to make sure each gesture is a contrast to the last.

Exercise 4.2

Try an on-the-spot 'hop, shuffle, down' step:

➤ *Hop* once on your right.

➤ When you land do a *shuffle* with your left foot: scuff the ground with the ball of your foot, forward and back quickly.

➤ Transfer the weight from right to left, putting your left foot *down* to prepare for the next 'hop, shuffle'.

➤ Repeat on the left.

➤ Repeat the whole cycle, getting quicker.

It is worth persevering with this work. No one picks up the steps immediately and everyone will benefit from repeating the exercises.

Once you have built the confidence of the group with these simple steps you can go on to develop more difficult ones but even if the work ends here the participants will be made aware of some key aspects of biomechanical training:

- the need for lightness of foot and balance;
- the support rhythm gives to the performer within an ensemble;
- the need to have all parts of the body working together.

WORK WITH STICKS

The basic skills developed here are precision, balance, coordination, rhythm, discipline and responsiveness.

In a way, the training with sticks is an extension of the tap dance, with the stick a kind of cane to complement the dance. In another sense, it is preparatory work for an actor in handling props. A third outcome of the work is to generate a strong feeling of ensemble. Work in a circle again, at least to begin with.

Exercise 4.3

➤ Take a stick like the one detailed in the 'What you will need' section and hold it vertically in your right hand about halfway down. Toss it to your left hand and catch it in the same place. Build this up so that everyone is throwing the sticks at the same time and to the same hands.

➤ Make sure your weight shifts accordingly from right to left and back. You can manipulate the circle in the same way as with the tap steps – making it larger, smaller, rotating individually, for example. Slowly the group will establish its own rhythm and with it a sense of collectivity.

➤ Now take the stick and hold it in your right hand about three quarters of the way down its length. Make sure your right foot is forward, your left foot back and that your feet are parallel – even though it feels unstable. Your feet should be spread far enough so that if you knelt on your back knee it would meet with the arch of your front foot.

➤ Toss the stick up so that it spins through 180 degrees and you can catch it at the other end. Try to make the stick feel 'soft'. Do not move your hand up to catch the stick, let it arrive softly back into your palm, as if it had never been thrown.

- ➤ Practice a number of times making sure that the impetus for the throw is in your legs.
- ➤ Swap hands and now make sure that your left leg is forward, still with parallel feet.
- ➤ Now repeat the whole sequence, throwing with your left hand.
- ➤ Then toss the stick from left to right with your feet shoulder-width apart keeping the 180 degree rotation.
- ➤ Repeat the same pattern – left, right and then left to right – for a 360-degree rotation (one whole revolution), then for one and a half and then two revolutions. This may take a few sessions.
- ➤ Now divide the actions of the throw into three, that is:

  - the 'preparation' for the throw or *otkaz*, which should be counted '*i*' (ee) – Russian for 'and';
  - the throw itself, the 'action' or *posil'* which can be counted '*ras*' (one);
  - the catching of the stick and the return to the starting point, the *tochka*, which should be counted '*dva*' (two).

As we will see this is the underlying rhythmic structure of all actions in biomechanics. It needs to be absorbed through practice rather than imposed on the work afterwards and therefore is best introduced at an early stage of the process.

The significance of this structure will become clear as the rest of the exercises are described, but it is worth noting here that if you have studied music – as we know Meyerhold did – then this kind of counting ('and', 'one', 'two') will not be unfamiliar to you.

'And' is the upbeat before any phrase of music. It's the sign a conductor gives you to get ready for the beginning of the music. In biomechanics this upbeat is visible in the physical frame of the actor as he prepares for the action itself. All the frozen runners in our Moscow workshop were effectively in thrall to the conductor's upbeat just as the participants of your workshop will be, once the convention of underscoring all the actions with '*i*, *ras*, *dva*' is set up!

'One' is the beginning of the phrase of music – when the bow begins to sound the strings of the violin. In biomechanics, 'one' is the action itself – either short or elongated. In the example of the Moscow workshop, the running itself constitutes the action. It is the release of energy following the freeze.

Finally, 'two' is the rest at the end of the phrase; not a full stop, only a pause, a moment of immobility which brings the energy of the action back under control again.

Now return to the throwing exercise, counting each part of the throw:

i	*otkaz*	the preparation to throw or a dipping in the legs
ras	*posil'*	the throwing itself
dva	*tochka*	the moment where all the force of the throw is brought back under control and the actor is once again balanced with the stick in the hand, ready to throw again.

FURTHER WORK WITH STICKS

Once the basics of the tripartite rhythm have been understood, you can go on to do many other things with the sticks. (Make sure you maintain a sense of fun while you are working as the inevitable dropped sticks, and bruises, can be a disincentive to continue.)

Exercise 4.4

➤ Balance the stick vertically on your flat palm making sure to use both your left and right hands.

➤ On the command 'hup', toss the stick from left to right while it is still balanced.

➤ Try balancing the stick on your arm, foot, knee, chin, shoulder.

➤ Sit and then lie down while you balance the stick on your palm – try to get both shoulder blades on the floor before you stand up again.

➤ Alternatively, walk across the room or in a circle while you balance the stick, changing direction and/or hands on the command of 'hup'.

➤ Or pair up and, holding hands, walk with your partner to the other side of the studio (it is doubly difficult to balance with two!). Try the same in threes and fours.

Exercise 4.5

Finally, in pairs:

➤ Stand a metre apart, holding your stick halfway down, and throw it vertically to your partner.

➤ Gradually increase the distance between you, while retaining the precision of the throw.

➤ Then, introduce another stick so that you have to throw and catch at the same time. In time, bring in a third and a fourth and find a pattern of throws to allow you to keep them all going at the same time.

➤ It's very rewarding when you are successful and depends on establishing a rhythmic understanding between the two of you. If you both count '*i, ras, dva*' together at first, it helps.

WORK WITH BALLS

The basic skills developed here are precision, coordination, rhythm, discipline, responsiveness and playfulness.

All the throwing exercises in the last section can also be done with tennis balls. These have the added advantage of encouraging a more immediate sense of playfulness. People can't resist throwing them around as soon as they are handed out! It's best to work with both sticks and balls, ringing the changes and mixing up the demands.

Exercise 4.6

➤ On your own, stand with your feet shoulder-width apart and facing forward and throw the ball from your left hand to your right in an arc above your head. Count the '*i, ras, dva*' rhythm as you throw. Make sure you bring the ball (and yourself) under control at the end of the throw.

➤ Now, move into a circle and take it in turns to throw the ball across the circle, concentrating again on the three parts of a biomechanical action. Make sure you make eye contact with your partner before you throw.

➤ Exaggerate, at first, the preparation for the throw so you can see physically what an *otkaz* looks like.

➤ Freeze after the throw to visualise the *tochka*.

➤ Your partner can do the same in receiving the throw – '*i*': preparation to catch, '*ras*': catch and '*dva*': freeze.

You are now caught in a kind of sculptural duet: the one in a gesture of throwing, the other in a gesture of catching. This could be the material for an improvisation based on the shapes created, or could be the first external clue to a character. Analyse which kind of characters are 'throwers' and which 'catchers'. Ask yourself who has the upper hand – is it always the thrower?

Exercise 4.7

➤   Still in a circle, and still only using one ball, throw the ball underarm with your right hand to the right hand of the person next to you (anticlockwise round the circle).

➤   The catcher then throws to the next person and so on, around the circle. The ball should never stop its smooth transition from one individual to the next. Imagine the ball is a ribbon around a huge birthday cake.

➤   Gradually, introduce another ball, and another, until there is at least one ball for every two participants arcing around the circle. Try to find the rhythm, the tempo which creates the smoothest journey for the ball.

➤   Then, start again going round the other way – from left hand to left hand, and clockwise round the circle. Build up in the same way to a number of balls.

➤   Finally, have half the balls going clockwise and half anticlockwise. Those who have a ball already can be skipped by the thrower so that the ball can continue its journey unimpeded.

➤   Continue the exercise until both the clockwise and the anticlockwise balls can glide effortlessly around the circle, almost as if the agents of this process were not there.

ÉTUDES

The basic skills developed here are precision, balance, coordination, efficiency, rhythm, expressiveness, responsiveness, discipline and playfulness.

I once asked Aleksei Levinski, one of two practising Russian masters of biomechanics, the question: What else does an actor need to do, beyond a training in the études? 'Nothing,' he said, 'that's all you need.'

Perfecting the five études gives you a comprehensive actor training, he argues, adding that a rudimentary training in biomechanics for the audience is also to be recommended!

In his biomechanical zeal Levinski may be overstressing the effectiveness of the études – it's difficult to see how the voice is trained through them, for instance. But at least in terms of the basic skills we have identified, he has a point. Whittled down from approximately twenty études in the 1920s, the five remaining ones develop all the key areas of an actor's physical craft. They have the following names:

1   'Throwing the Stone'
2   'Shooting the Bow'
3   'The Slap'
4   'The Stab with the Dagger'
5   'The Leap to the Chest'.

The first two are solo études and the remaining three are studies for two actors. We will focus on the pair étude, 'The Slap', which of all the studies demonstrates the key skills most clearly.

'THE SLAP'

First, look at the individual actions that go together to make up the entire étude.

It may not look it but 'The Slap' is the least complex of the five etudes, partly because much of the material is repeated. However, there are three important points to remember:

1   There is no direct physical contact – the 'slap' is rather like the kind you see in silent movies or in (very stagey) fights in the theatre, with the passive 'victim' making the sound of the slap as the 'aggressor' swipes close to the face.
2   The actors work together, with the *active* performer setting the rhythm of the étude. The pair effectively becomes a 'mini ensemble' with the hierarchy being inverted halfway through.
3   Each action is a 'building block', a small part of the overall action 'to slap'. At the same time each action is itself made up of three sub-actions (*otkaz*, *posil'*, *tochka*) and these go together to create the rhythm of the piece.

Exercise 4.8

➤ Two actors face each other approximately one metre apart.
Dactyl

Figure 4.1 Neutral stance

Figure 4.2 Leap to the stance

Figure 4.3 Preparation to shake (hands)

Figure 4.4 Shake

Figure 4.5 Neutral stance

Figure 4.6 Tap dance

Figure 4.7 Leap to the stance

➤ Pair splits into active (a) and passive (b).

Figure 4.8 (a) Preparation to slap (b) Cowering

Figure 4.9 (a) Taking aim (b) Offering the cheek

Figure 4.10 (a) The slap (aggressor) (b) The slap (victim)

➤ Passive and active swap on the move to Neutral stance.

Figure 4.11 Neutral stance

Figure 4.12 Tap dance

Figure 4.13 Leap to the stance

Figure 4.14 (a) Cowering (b) Preparation to slap

Figure 4.15 (a) Offering the cheek (b) Taking aim

Figure 4.16 (a) The slap (victim) (b) The slap (aggressor)

➤ Together again.

Figure 4.17 Neutral stance

Figure 4.18 Preparation to shake

Figure 4.19 Shake

Figure 4.20 Parade

Dactyl

Huge mistakes have been made in the past when actors and directors have tried to reconstruct these études from pictures and prose descriptions without an understanding of this *rhythm*. In recent years the video archives of Levinski and Bogdanov have eliminated most of these problems as they show the actor moving, but it is still worth noting that any training with the études is worthless if this key aspect of the work is not understood.

WORKING ON THE ÉTUDE

To understand fully this question of rhythm we have to return to the tripartite structure first encountered with the stick work.

Looking again at the photographs in Figures 4.1–4.20 which give the overall order of these actions, imagine that each image is the 'end point' of the action, the *tochka*. Thus each action is preceded by an *otkaz*, the preparation and by the *posil'*, the action itself. Let's take the following as an example:

Preparation to shake (hands) (Figure 4.3)

You have leapt to the position in Figure 4.2 and now are standing with your left foot forward and your right foot back, with your feet parallel and your arms by your sides. (It's the same position you adopted when throwing the stick with your left hand.) Your weight should be evenly spread across both feet. Now make a small movement forward with your right shoulder in the opposite direction you are about to travel in – this is the *otkaz*.

Now send your shoulder backwards and rotate your feet through ninety degrees. At the same time bring your right arm back, bending at the elbow to make a shaking gesture. Your left arm is straight in front of you and you are looking down it. All the weight is now on your right leg. This is the *posil'* and can be counted by the leader as a long '*raaaaaaaaaaaaaaaaaaaaaas*'.

When this action comes to a rest and the body is controlled and stationary you have reached the end point of the movement, the *tochka*, marked by the call of '*dva*'. You should now be in the position of Figure 4.3.

This action can first be practised in a circle with everyone looking in. Ultimately, though, it is best worked on in a pair, facing each other about a metre apart, with one member of the duet (the *active* one) setting the rhythm of the action. The rest of the main actions of the étude, then, conform to this structure, as shown below.

Name yourselves (a) and (b) and note that all the (a) and (b) actions are performed simultaneously.

Shake ([a] and [b] together) (Figure 4.4)

Otkaz: A dip in the legs.
Posil':   The right hand and arm extend forward and down, the hand keeping the shape of the handshake. The left arm goes back and is bent at the elbow, acting as a counterpoint to the right. All the weight shifts to the left foot. The hands clasp.
Tochka: Hold the shake.

Preparation to slap (Figure 4.8 [a])

Otkaz: A small movement forward with your right shoulder.
Posil':   Rotate the feet through ninety degrees. The right hand arcs up and back, the palm opening out and pausing above the head. The left arm is extended out in front and you are looking down the arm again.
Tochka: Hold the position.

Cowering (Figure 4.8 [b])

Otkaz: A small movement forward with your right shoulder.
Posil':   Shift the weight on to the right foot, with your right arm hanging down. Look over your left shoulder without extending the arm out.
Tochka: Hold the cower.

Taking aim (Figure 4.9 [a])

Otkaz: A dip in the legs.
Posil':   Bring the right hand down and forward, to meet with the cheek of your partner, simultaneously rotating the feet to face forward again. Your left arm should again counter the right and extend backwards. Your arms will form a zigzag. Your weight should shift to the left foot.
Tochka: Hold the position.

Offering the cheek (Figure 4.9 [b])

Otkaz: A dip in the legs.

Posil':   Leaning towards your partner, bring both hands up to just under the chin, ready to clap, simultaneously rotating the feet to face forward again. Your weight should shift to the left foot.

Tochka: Hold the position.

The slap (aggressor) (Figure 4.10 [a])

Otkaz: Your right hand comes quickly back to the position of 8(a). The rhythm is like the back-swing in tennis before hitting the ball.

Posil':   The right hand comes quickly down to just next to the cheek of your partner. It pauses momentarily before you bend forward, looking down, resting your right elbow on your left knee, with your left arm up behind you. All the weight has shifted to the left side.

Tochka: Hold the bent position.

The slap (victim) (Figure 4.10 [b])

Otkaz: A dip in the legs and a bringing up of the hands ready to clap in a downwards direction.

Posil':   Simultaneously, as your partner brings his hand to your cheek, clap your hands downwards, take your left hand to the left side of your face, straighten and shift the weight to the back foot (the right). Your back will now be arched and the upper part of the left arm should be perfectly vertical, pushing your head back further. Your right arm is hanging down relaxed behind.

Tochka: (Momentarily) hold the position!

Now let's look at the other actions: Dactyl, Leap to the stance, Tap dance and Parade.

Dactyl (Not shown)

The dactyl begins and ends each étude. It gathers the performer's attention together and sets a rhythmic pattern for the rest of the exercise.

Stand with your feet shoulder-width apart and your arms relaxed by your side. Your knees should be slightly bent – soft – so that your body is as responsive as possible. Slowly lean forward so that you can feel your toes taking the strain a little. Bend your knees further and bring your arms back. It might feel like a swimmer getting ready to dive into an Olympic pool.

Then raise your arms above your head, straighten your legs and come on to your toes, all in the same action. Let your arms bend and your elbows travel towards your hips. When your arms are parallel with the floor and your back is bowed you can clap downwards and as sharply as possible, twice. The rest of the body bounces in time with this double handclap. Finally, return to neutral with your arms by your sides (Figure 4.1).

Note that this action is counted differently: all the preparatory actions up to the moment where the hands are above the head are an *otkaz*, counted '*i*'. The two handclaps are then counted '*ras*, *dva*' in quick succession. Nevertheless, the tripartite structure remains.

Leap to the stance (Figure 4.2)

This is a deceptively difficult action and not easy to commit to paper, so do refer to the video archives listed in the Bibliography – Gennadi Bogdanov's German video (1997), issued by the Mime Centrum in Berlin, is now available in English and shows two biomechanically trained actors performing 'The Slap' in its entirety.

From neutral, bend in the same way as for the beginning of the dactyl. Then, following the upward movement of your arms, jump up, parting your legs and, now, pointing your arms down, so that you land facing forward with both feet parallel. Your left foot is forward and the right is back. (Again, this is the same position for throwing the stick with the left hand.)

As you land, your arms pivot at the elbow and come up from the downwards position to end up parallel with the floor. Your head comes up almost to meet your arms as your whole body softens the landing. Slowly unfurl to neutral.

Tap dance (Figure 4.12)

If you have mastered the 'hop, shuffle, down' step on page 121, perform this step opposite your partner while waving your arms around above your head. The gesture can resemble washing your hands and arms!

If not, skip merrily in tandem so that the étude is punctuated with a very different rhythm. You can still do the arm gestures.

Parade (Figure 4.20)

As the finale before the dactyl, both of you circle the space, arm in arm, walking briskly in a jaunty, Chaplin-like waddle. Your outside arm can scythe the air with a mechanical flourish.

The *active* actor at the conclusion halts the action and steps aside in readiness for both actors to perform the dactyl standing alongside each other.

BACK TO THE BASIC SKILLS

Now let's return to the key skills listed on pp. 112–17 and see exactly how 'The Slap' develops what Levinski calls 'all you need' as an actor:

PRECISION

Work on the étude is repetitive. The aim of the exercise is to mimic perfectly the physical shape of 'The Slap' as it has been passed down from generation to generation. This necessarily makes demands on your ability to remember the gestures and to reproduce them to a very fine degree of accuracy.

BALANCE

You will soon see as you practise these movements that keeping your feet parallel is unnatural and that you need to work harder physically to maintain your balance. As with the stick work and tap steps, your weight is constantly being shifted from left to right and this tests your ability to keep balanced.

COORDINATION

When you are engaged in biomechanical work, all of your muscles are at work at the same time. While your arms are moving in one direction your feet and legs will be doing something else. At the same time 'The Slap' demands a high level of coordination with your partner, so that you are both working together like two cogs in a bigger machine.

EFFICIENCY

This is a bit of a misnomer. It's obvious that if you wanted to slap someone without wasting any energy you would not engage in all the elaborate playfulness of the étude 'The Slap'. But given that you are performing in a consciously *theatrical* environment in Meyerhold's world (far removed from any naturalistic behaviour), your extended gestures and large characterisations have to be sustainable. The études therefore embody some (not all) of the key aspects of machine-like efficiency, such as *fluidity*, *smoothness*, *strict organisation* and *accurate repetition*.

RHYTHM

Work on the étude encourages the actor to embody at a deep level the tripartite rhythm of biomechanics – *otkaz*, *posil'* and *tochka*. Thus, the actor is prepared both at an individual level (a gesture or movement) and at a general level (the structure of an act or a whole play) to engage physically with the rhythmic challenges set by the director.

EXPRESSIVENESS

The extended and exaggerated gestures of the étude are a kind of symbol of the type of heightened theatricality Meyerhold was pursuing in his theatre. Not that these gestures are brought directly on to stage – it is highly inadvisable simply to 'quote' the étude while working on a play – but the same *kind* of mobile, elongated and dynamic style of expression is appropriate when applying this training to work on text.

RESPONSIVENESS

As a pair étude, 'The Slap' is particularly good at developing the unspoken understanding between actors which underpins all good ensemble work. As the rhythm of the étude is set by the *active* actor, it is imperative that his choices of tempo are 'read' by the *passive* actor and responded to in the moment of performing. This *responsibility* is, of course, shared as passive and active swap halfway through, reminding us of the collective spirit which underlies all of the work.

PLAYFULNESS AND DISCIPLINE

A glance back at the list of actions which make up 'The Slap' might clarify the balance of playfulness and discipline in this particular étude. After shaking hands in a slow, ritualistic manner, the two performers dance opposite one another, before one slaps the other in the face. They then celebrate this exchange with a further dance, followed by a slap in reply and a final flourish (the parade). Both the dances and the parade offer an explicit rhythmic and stylistic counterpoint to the slower, more deliberate ritual of slapping.

IMPROVISATION EXERCISES

This section will show how to enhance what you have learnt by using music; extending the sticks and balls work; extending the étude work; and reconstructing an existing étude.

The work thus far is perhaps best thought of as preparation (an *otkaz* in itself!). The skills-based exercises provide the building blocks for the rest of the practice, rather like the study of études in music – developing in the performer an understanding of the technical demands of the art form. But exercises in music and études in biomechanics do not in themselves make a creative work. That is the domain of the director and actor in a different relationship – where the *individual* skills of a performer can come to the fore, even within a sharply defined ensemble.

USING MUSIC

The beginning of the process can be signed by the introduction of music to some of the earlier exercises. Asking an actor to perform a learned étude to different kinds of music brings a different level of complexity to the work. It personalises the work in a way, as the responses to the music emerge from within the actor, even if the external form of the étude remains the same. Meyerhold's favourite accompaniment was Chopin, but any music will do providing the following things are understood:

- Do not simply mimic the rhythms of the music in your performance.
- Make sure you work against, as well as with, the direction of the music, at different times.
- Retain the music inside you, even if the external musical stimulus is lost later on.

Moving to musical stimuli also marks an important shift from exercises called by the leader to personally motivated action, stimulated by a sound cue.

If I have a preference regarding the kind of music to use it is for *jazz*, a form which is so variegated in its many guises that you are never short of stimulating material. If you have no immediate ideas yourself try some Dixieland (early Louis Armstrong, for example) and then contrast this with Charlie Mingus.

Exercise 4.9

- ➤ Listen to the music first and then watch selected pairs perform the étude with the music.
- ➤ Get them to perform again and to make different choices.
- ➤ Observe, when *active* and *passive* change, how this affects the rhythmic responses to the music.
- ➤ Put on a contrasting piece and compare the performance.
- ➤ Analyse when the pair are working with the music and when they are working against it.
- ➤ Consider the effectiveness of each strategy.
- ➤ Finally, get the pair to perform without the music.
- ➤ See if they can retain a quality of the music in their performance.

EXTENDING THE STICKS AND BALLS WORK

As the warm-up for this chapter indicated, skills-based work can always diversify into improvisation and this includes the work with sticks and balls. Moving into improvisation is one way of getting to understand how to share a 'trick' with the audience and continues the idea introduced above of individualising or personalising the skills.

Exercise 4.10

➤ Try balancing other things: chairs, small tables, even other actors.
➤ Take three movable pieces of furniture and improvise the most imaginative way of 'setting' them on stage, in full view of the audience. Be sure to use the same kinds of skills developed in the stick work – balance, precision, coordination – but add in a sense of playfulness.
➤ Do the same exercise to transform from one scene to another.
➤ Play these improvisations with set and props in different rhythms.
➤ Dream up scenarios in which objects are exchanged, or thrown from one person to another.
➤ Work on these as 'routines' in pairs or threes, so that the trick of exchanging is perfected.
➤ Possible contexts could be:

The dinner party	The schoolroom
The jail breakout	Setting up camp
The funeral procession	The building site

➤ Build up these routines to include more performers, but do not lose the discipline and precision of the work as the level of improvisation increases.
➤ Have a 'conversation' of ball-throwing with your partner.
➤ Toss the balls between you in different ways and with different qualities.
➤ Allow the 'dialogue' to emerge naturally from these different ball exchanges.
➤ Be sure to resist the obvious and go against the grain – play a love scene, for example, as you hurl the balls at each other.
➤ Play the same scene without the balls but retain the quality of action (throw) and reaction (catch).

EXTENDING THE ÉTUDE WORK

In some quarters it may be considered heresy to rework the études in any way. Clearly there is good reason to keep the existing études as they are. At the very least, the five études provide a link with Meyerhold in some way and they are evidently effective when it comes to developing a Meyerholdian style of performance.

But without abandoning the principles of biomechanics, it is possible to generate improvisation work around the études which at its most extreme might involve the development of new études. There is nothing problematic about this if such work is viewed as part of a journey towards a fully fledged biomechanical performance – one that observes the principles of biomechanics without simply aping its external forms. Developing an étude of one's own may then be seen as part of the process of becoming an autonomous actor, an essential progression in any case.

If you want to create your own étude, first analyse the nature of the études which exist. Here's a start:

- They all begin and end with a dactyl.
- They all involve some kind of protagonist–antagonist structure and weaponry of one sort or another. (For the solo études the antagonist is imagined – either shot at with a bow or the reluctant receiver of a stone! For the pair études, the structure is more obvious.)
- They are all underpinned by the *otkaz*, *posil'*, *tochka* rhythm.
- They all subdivide a large action into separate 'building blocks'.

Take these similarities and create a minute-long, solo étude which conforms to these conventions.

Exercise 4.11

➤ Think of a title first, for example 'Shooting the Catapult'.
➤ Break the overall action down into fifteen to twenty sub-actions.
➤ Choreograph each sub-action with a sensitivity to the style of 'the Slap':

– use elongated, exaggerated gestures;
– shift the weight from left to right and from the upper body to the lower body;
– clearly delineate the *otkaz*, *posil'* and *tochka* for each sub-action;
– make sure the whole body is involved.

> ➤   Memorise the work so that you can teach it to someone else.
> ➤   Do the same but this time for a pair étude, 'the Kick' for example.
> ➤   Record your étude using a stills camera and/or a video camera. Try to imagine that your recording might serve as a record for someone else, perhaps another eighty years later, to reconstruct your work.

Now you have as many études as you have group members and this can be a rich resource for discussion and further practice. First, comparing the études will help the group see the underlying pattern to the existing biomechanical études. Second, it will help uncover an element of the creative process Meyerhold and his contemporaries went through in the 1920s. Third, it will be clear which kind of action works and which should be rejected. A pair étude which is simply aggressive or violent – something like 'The Blow to the Head' for example – will patently fail to capture the quality of 'The Slap' as recorded above. Meyerhold's études, and by extension his theatre, depended on a mixture of emotions and of atmosphere – that was why he often called it *grotesque*.

RECONSTRUCTIONS

A parallel exercise associated with the études involves *reconstruction*. Instead of creating your own études based on the pattern above, the aim is to recreate an existing étude – one which you haven't worked on – from scratch. This is particularly useful if you use different sources, so that part of the learning is about how Meyerhold's études have evolved. It is advisable to do this exercise after the group has had some experience of 'The Slap', so that the form and purpose of the work are understood. This will inevitably affect how the reconstructions are performed – the tripartite rhythm will always influence the performances, but there is little point in having a 'control group' operating in a vacuum.

The exercise is made possible by the wide range of different sources documenting the études. These span an eighty-year period from the early 1920s to today and thus the exercise of reconstruction is also a way of physicalising history. Of all the études 'Shooting the Bow' has been documented most comprehensively.

Exercise 4.12

➤ Split the group into pairs or threes and give each group one of the following sources:

1 Robert Leach's prose description of the 'mime' 'Shooting from the Bow' (printed in Leach 1989: 63).

2 Erast Garin's prose description of 'Shooting the Bow' (reprinted in Schmidt 1996: 38).

3 Eugenio Barba's and Nicola Savarese's diagrammatic reconstructions of Garin's description (Barba and Savarese 1991: 102).

4 Robert Leach's list of actions describing the étude 'Shooting from the Bow' (printed in Hodge 2000: 49–50).

5 (Separately) the accompanying diagrams (in Hodge 2000: 51).

6 An undisclosed contemporary student's description of 'Shooting with Bow and Arrow' (reprinted in Law and Gordon 1996: 120–2).

7 Another contemporary description of 'Shooting with Bow and Arrow' by P. Urbanovich (also reprinted in Law and Gordon 1996: 122–3).

8 The collection of photographs showing Nikolai Kustov performing the étude 'Shooting the Bow' (reprinted in Zarrilli 1995: 94–5).

9 (Separately) the accompanying prose description (in Zarrilli 1995: 93–4).

10 Aleksei Levinski's video record of the étude 'Shooting the Bow' (Levinski 1995).

11 Gennadi Bogdanov's video record of the étude 'Shooting the Bow' (Bogdanov 1997).

➤ Give each group thirty minutes to reconstruct the étude from their particular source.

➤ Make sure each group works independently and resists the temptation to 'add in' material from outside.

➤ Perform each étude and (if you want) video the overall outcomes, so that a deeper, more prolonged analysis of the results can be held.

The sources can roughly be organised into four types: prose descriptions, diagrams, photos and video records. The first point of analysis may, then, centre around the relationship between the different kinds of documentation and the final reconstruction. So we could ask ourselves the following questions: Is it inevitable that the pictorial forms of documentation give a more 'accurate' feeling of the étude? How do we measure what is accurate and what isn't? Can you organise the études differently, in terms of their level of complexity, for example? Does this give us a clue to their date?

In general the étude has become more complex as it has evolved, but Levinski and Bogdanov's versions from the 1990s still remain very close to the pictorial sources from the 1920s and 1930s. This may not be surprising as their teacher was none other than Nikolai Kustov!

A final question which must at some stage be asked is: What does the individual performer bring to the étude? Or, put another way: To what extent can we see the soul of the actor embodied in the external shapes of the étude?

WORK ON TEXT

The last question offers a good springboard into this concluding section, for it is ultimately the soul of the actor – the inner understanding, if you like – which takes the work beyond training and into creative work on text.

There is an implicit warning here for any performer who has worked in biomechanics: remember the 'bio' (the *living* organism) as well as the 'mechanics' and make sure that the external forms of the training are fully integrated into your person. Otherwise, you will only be quoting Meyerhold in the manner of an essay, rather than working organically with his principles on your own terms.

It is not my intention here to go over Meyerhold's directorial approach again – we have seen the fruits of his approach to text in Chapter 3 in the production analysis of *The Government Inspector*. My aim is more simple in this section: simply to offer one moment of contact between the training and the move towards production. This necessarily includes an element of adaptation which is very much in the spirit of Meyerhold's notion of the director-author.

THEATRICALISING THE GROTESQUE

Read the following Icelandic short story 'Now I Should Laugh, If I Were Not Dead' (from Carter 1990: 102–3):

Once two married women had a dispute about which of their husbands was the biggest fool. At last they agreed to try [and see] if they were as foolish as they seemed to be. One of the women then played this trick. When her husband came home from his work, she took a spinning wheel and carders, and sitting down, began to card and spin, but neither the farmer nor anyone else saw any wool in her hands. Her husband, observing this, asked if she was mad to scrape the teazles together and spin the wheel, without having the wool and prayed to her to tell what this meant. She said it was scarcely to be expected that he should see what she was doing, for it was a kind of linen too fine to be seen by the eye. Of this she was going to make him clothes. He thought this a very good explanation, and wondered much at how clever his good wife was, and was not a little glad in looking forward to the joy and pride he would feel in having on these marvellous clothes. When his wife had spun, as she said, enough for the clothes, she set up the loom, and wove the stuff. Her husband used, now and then, to visit her, wondering at the skill of his good lady. She was much amused at all this, and made haste to carry out the trick well. She took the cloth from the loom, when it was finished, and first washed and fulled it, and last, sat down to work cutting it and sewing the clothes out of it. When she had finished all this, she bade her husband come and try the clothes on, but did not dare let him put them on alone, wherefore she would help him. So she made believe to dress him in his fine clothes, and although the poor man was in reality naked, yet he firmly believed that it was all his own mistake, and thought his clever wife had made him these wondrous-fine clothes, and so glad he was at this, that he could not help jumping about for joy.

Now we return to the other wife. When her husband came home from his work, she asked him why in the world he was up, and going about upon his feet. The man was startled at this question, and said: 'Why on earth do you ask this?' She persuaded him that he was very ill, and told him he had better go to bed. He believed this, and went to bed as soon as he could. When some time had passed, the wife said she would do the last services for him. He asked why, and prayed her by all means not to do so. She said: 'Why do you behave like a fool: don't you know you died this morning? I am going, at once, to have your coffin made.' Now the poor man, believing this to be true, rested thus till he was put into his coffin. His wife then appointed a day for the burial, and hired six coffin-carriers, and asked the other couple to follow her dear husband to his grave. She had a window made in one side of the coffin, so that her husband might see all that passed round him. When the hour came for removing the coffin, the naked man came there, thinking that everyone would admire his delicate clothes. But far from it; although the coffin bearers were in a sad mood, yet nobody could help laughing when they saw this naked fool. And when the man in the coffin caught a glance of him, he cried out as loud as he could: 'Now I should laugh, if I were not dead!' The burial was put off, and the man was let out of the coffin.

Now consider how you might stage the story in the spirit of Meyerhold, focusing on the following:

* *Stylisation*: How do you pare down the story to its essence and build from there? It's already very simple but you need to identify those elements which cannot be lost without losing the story itself.
* *Restrictions*: Allow yourselves a specified time to make the work and restrict everything to the use of two chairs and a few of the metre-long sticks.
* *Double narrative*: Think about how to tell both stories; you could, for example, split into two and work on each of the wives' stories separately.
* *Montage*: Having divided the story up, how do you put it together again? Think about the overall performance as a *montage* of smaller elements and find imaginative ways of cutting from one story to the other. Think of each piece of material as if they were discrete actions of 'The Slap' – building blocks which need assembling into a theatrical whole.
* *Characterisation*: Define the main characters of the story. Think about them in purely physical terms: how do you think they look or move, and what external idiosyncrasies might they have? How can you begin to embody the characters, working from the outside? Which muscle groups are prominent in the make-up of this character? How might they travel across the stage? Have in the back of your mind the rhythms and shapes of the étude, but don't allow these to dominate – the character comes first but may have the residue of the stylised movements associated with 'The Slap'.
* *Use of props*: Which objects are indispensable in the story and how can you create them with very limited materials? Remember the work with sticks and the extension of these exercises towards an imaginative kind of play with props.
* *The grotesque*: Spend at least a third of your time working on the ensemble scene at the end of the story. Crucially how do you *trans-form*, physically, from the mournful atmosphere of the 'funeral' to

the unsuppressed hilarity of the conclusion? Identify who is the agent, the stimulus, for this transformation – is it the wives, the arrival of the naked husband, the coffin-bound man, or 'some devilish hand' from outside? Again, the transformation might have the quality of a long-drawn-out *posil'* from the étude. But it might just as well be a snap metamorphosis from one picture to another.

• *Active and passive*: Finally, analyse where the power lies at specific moments in the adaptation. Imagine the performance is a larger version of 'The Slap' and that at any one point someone is *active* and the rest are *passive* – not in the sense of being mute or marginalized, but in the biomechanical sense of being responsive to the rhythmic offerings of the *active* member. This will add definition and focus to the work and allow you to determine the direction of the ensemble at any moment.

Now view the work and (if you can) film it. The external eye of the video camera can be a very helpful aid in evaluating how successful the training has been. It also allows you, as participants, to view yourselves from 'outside' and to analyse where the work has impacted on your practice.

CONCLUSIONS

There should be no predetermined outcomes when working with biomechanics – the best work will emerge organically from a continuing process of training, experimentation and performance. Always avoid the temptation to reveal your training directly to an audience. If you have worked seriously through the exercises in this chapter and applied yourself, if you have spent time reflecting on the practice and been prepared to invest some of your unique individuality (your soul) in the work, then the results of your training will be more than evident in the final analysis – the moment of performance.

This may be in terms very closely connected to Meyerhold – you might now want to take part in one of the plays he directed and work closely in the style of production we have encountered in this book. You might on the other hand choose a different direction. But even in the most contrasting of theatrical environments, in the low-key world of Naturalism, for example, the training described here will be invaluable. Mainly because of its attention to the *basic skills* of acting.

Meyerhold understood that the demands made on the actor were multiple and complex. But he was also aware of the common ground shared between all performers and attempted to cover that ground with his holistic actor training.

Above all, his workshop was a space for *learning*, not just for the participants but for all those involved in the training. As Erast Garin, his star pupil, put it:

> Everyone learned [in Meyerhold's studio] – students and teachers alike. It was a laboratory for working through the foundations of a new aesthetic.
>
> (Leach 1994: 105)

If the same can be said of your own workshop experience then you will have learnt the most valuable lesson of all from Meyerhold's training.

Now, let's conclude with a final practical exercise.

Exercise 4.13

➤   Gather in a circle about a metre apart from each other
➤   Perform a dactyl
➤   Turn to your left or right and face your partner
➤   Leap to the stance
➤   Prepare to shake
➤   Shake

and depart. . . .

BIBLIOGRAPHY

BOOKS AND ARTICLES

Banham, Martin (ed.) (1992) *The Cambridge Guide to Theatre*, Cambridge: Cambridge University Press.

Bann, Stephen (ed.) (1974) *The Tradition of Constructivism*, New York: Da Capo.

Barba, Eugenio and Savarese, Nicola (1991) *A Dictionary of Theatre Anthropology: The Secret Art of the Performer*, trans. Richard Fowler, London: Routledge.

Benedetti, Jean (1990) *Stanislavski: A Biography*, London: Methuen.

Braun, Edward (1991) *Meyerhold on Theatre*, London: Methuen.

—— (1995) *A Revolution in Theatre*, London: Methuen.

Brecht, Bertolt (1978) *Brecht on Theatre*, trans. John Willett, London: Methuen.

Carter, Angela (ed.) (1990) *The Virago Book of Fairy Tales*, London: Virago Press.

Chekhov, Anton (1991) *Plays*, trans. Michael Frayn, London: Methuen.

Clurman, Harold (1998) 'An Excerpt from Harold Clurman's Unpublished Diary', *Theater* 28(2): 79–80.

Deák, Frantisek (1982) 'Meyerhold's Staging of Sister Beatrice', *The Drama Review* 26(1): 41–50.

Eisenstein, Sergei (1988) *Writings: Vol 1, 1922–1934*, trans. and ed. Richard Taylor, London: British Film Institute.

Fitzpatrick, Sheila (1982) *The Russian Revolution 1917–1932*, Oxford: Oxford University Press.

Forsyth, James (1977) *Listening to the Wind: An Introduction to Alexander Blok*, Oxford: William A. Meeuws.

Frost, Anthony and Yarrow, Ralph (1990) *Improvisation in Drama*, London: Macmillan.

Gladkov, Aleksandr (1997) *Meyerhold Speaks, Meyerhold Rehearses*, trans. Alma Law, London: Harwood Academic Publishers.

Gogol, Nikolai (1980) *The Theater of Nikolay Gogol*, trans. and intro. Milton Ehre, Chicago, Ill.: University Press of Chicago.

—— (1997) *The Government Inspector*, trans. Steven Mulrine, London: Nick Hern Books.

Gordon, Mel (1995) 'Meyerhold's Biomechanics', in Philip Zarrilli (ed.) *Acting (Re)Considered*, London: Routledge.

Green, Michael (ed.) (1986) *Russian Symbolist Theatre*, Ann Arbor, Mich.: Ardis.

Hawkins-Dady, Mark (1987) 'Gogol's "The Government Inspector" at the National Theatre, 1985', *New Theatre Quarterly* 3(12): 358–76.

Hodge, Alison (ed.) (2000) *Twentieth Century Actor Training*, London: Routledge.

Hoffmann, E.T.A. (1982) *Tales of Hoffmann*, trans. R.J. Hollingdale, London: Penguin Classics.

Hoover, Marjorie L. (1974) *Meyerhold: The Art of Conscious Theater*, Amherst, Mass.: University of Massachusetts Press.

Houghton, Norris (1938) *Moscow Rehearsals*, London: George Allen & Unwin.

Ibsen, Henrik (1980) *Plays: Two*, trans. Michael Meyer, London: Methuen.

Law, Alma (1982) 'The Magnanimous Cuckold', *The Drama Review* 26(1), Spring: 61–86.

—— and Gordon, Mel (1996) *Meyerhold, Eisenstein and Biomechanics*, London: McFarland.

Leach, Robert (1989) *Vsevolod Meyerhold*, Cambridge: Cambridge University Press.

—— (1994) *Revolutionary Theatre*, London: Routledge.

—— (2000) 'Meyerhold and Biomechanics', in Alison Hodge (ed.) *Twentieth Century Actor Training*, London: Routledge.

Lunacharsky, A.V. (1978) 'Gogol-Meyerhold's "The Inspector General"', *October* 7, Winter: 57–70.

Magarshack, David (1957) *Gogol: A Life*, London: Faber & Faber.

—— (1986) *Stanislavsky: A Life*, London: Faber.

Mayakovsky, Vladimir (1995) *Mayakovsky: Plays*, trans. Guy Daniels, Evanston, Ill.: Northwestern University Press.

Nemirovich-Danchenko, Vladimir (1968) *My Life in the Russian Theatre*, trans. John Cournos, New York: Theatre Arts Books.

Pavlov, Ivan (1927) *Conditioned Reflexes: An Investigation of the Physiological Activity of the Cerebral Cortex*, trans. G.V. Anrep, New York: Dover Publications.

Pérez Sánchez, Alfonso E. and Gállego, Julián (1995) *Goya: The Complete Etchings and Lithographs*, Munich: Prestel-Verlag.

Pitches, Jonathan (2000) 'Theatre, Science and the Spirit of the Time: Towards a Physics of Performance', in Anthony Frost (ed.) *Theatre Theories from Plato to Virtual Reality*, Norwich: EAS.

Pitches, Jonathan and Shrubsall, Anthony (1997) 'Two Perspectives on the Phenomenon of Biomechanics in Contemporary Performance: An Account of Gogol's "Government Inspector" in Production', *Studies in Theatre Production* 16: 93–128.

Rudlin, John (1994) *Commedia dell'Arte: An Actor's Handbook*, London: Routledge.

Rudnitsky, Konstantin (1981) *Meyerhold The Director*, trans. George Petrov, Ann Arbor, Mich.: Ardis.

—— (1988) *Russian and Soviet Theatre*, trans. Roxane Permar, London: Thames & Hudson.

Schmidt, Paul (ed.) (1996) *Meyerhold at Work*, New York: Applause.

—— (1998) 'Acting Music, Scoring Text', *Theater*, 28(2): 81–5.

Schuler, Catherine (1996) *Women in Russian Theatre: The Actress in the Silver Age*, London: Routledge.

Stanislavsky, Constantin (1980) *My Life in Art*, trans. J.J. Robbins, London: Methuen.

Symons, James M. (1971) *Meyerhold's Theatre of the Grotesque: Post Revolutionary Productions, 1920–1932*, Coral Gables, Fla.: University of Miami Press.

Taylor, Frederick Winslow (1947) *Scientific Management*, New York: Harper & Row.

Worrall, Nick (1972) 'Meyerhold Directs Gogol's "Government Inspector"', *Theatre Quarterly* 2: 75–95.

—— (1982) *Nikolai Gogol and Ivan Turgenev*, London: Macmillan.

Zarrilli, Phillip (ed.) (1995) *Acting (Re)Considered*, London: Routledge.

Zhdanov, Andrei (1977) *Soviet Writers Congress 1934*, London: Lawrence & Wishart.

FILMS AND VIDEOS

Bogdanov, Gennadi (1997) *Meyerhold's Theater and Biomechanics*, Berlin: Mime Centrum (video).

—— (1998) *Meyerhold's Biomechanics and Rhythm*, 6 Volumes, Exeter: Arts Documentation Unit (video).

—— and Raüke, Ralf (1995) *Meyerhold's Throwing the Stone*, Exeter: Arts Documentation Unit (video).

Chaplin, Charlie (dir.) (1936) *Modern Times*, 87 minutes (film).

Eisenstein, Sergei (dir.) (1928) *October*, 90 minutes (film).

Levinski, Aleksei (1995) *Meyerhold's Biomechanics: A Workshop*, Exeter: Arts Documentation Unit (video).

INDEX

active 127, 131, 133–4, 138, 142, 144–5, 153; *see also* passive
Aeschylus: *Oresteia* 100
Aleksandrinsky Theatre 12, 22, 27–8, 83
Alpers, Boris 34, 104
Antoine, André 10
Aristophanes 53
Aristotle 92
Armstrong, Louis 145

balance 19, 76, 112–14, 120–2, 124, 126, 142, 146
Barba, Eugenio 149
Bely, Andrei 17
biomechanics 26, 32–3, 37–8, 42, 46, 60, 67–73, 75–6, 102, 104–8, 112, 114, 117–18, 120, 123, 126–7, 143–4, 147, 150, 153; *see also* étude
Blok, Aleksandr 16–21, 23, 26–7, 30, 62–3; *Fairground Booth (Balaganchik)* 16, 18–20, 27, 62–3

Bogdanov, Gennadi 38, 42, 98, 117, 138, 141, 149–50
Braun, Edward 32, 43; *Meyerhold on Theatre* 43, 45
Brecht, Bertolt 3

Chaplin, Charlie 37, 44, 46, 73–6, 102, 104, 108, 116, 142; *Modern Times* 76
Chekhov, Anton 5–6, 8–10, 12, 47, 49–50, 56; *Cherry Orchard* 9–10, 47; *Seagull* 5–6, 9, 47, 49; *Three Sisters* 47; *Wedding* 9
Chekhov, Michael 44, 103
Chopin, Frédérik 56–7, 67, 145
Clurman, Harold 109
commedia dell'arte 18–21, 23, 25–7, 32, 34, 37, 58–9, 62, 68, 70–1, 73, 93, 115, 117
Constructivism 33–7, 39
coordination 70, 112–14, 120, 122, 125–6, 143, 146
Crommelynk, Fernand: *Magnanimous Cuckold* 34, 37, 105

Deák, Frantisek 14
discipline 12, 26, 57, 67, 70,
    105–6, 112–14, 116, 120, 122,
    125–6, 144, 146; see also
    playfulness
Dostoevsky, Fyodor 82
Dramatichesky Theatre 12, 16, 25
Dr Dapertutto 23–7, 63, 65, 83
Dumas, Alexander: Lady of the
    Camellias 56

efficiency 33, 112, 114, 126, 143
Eisenstein, Sergei 30, 38, 46, 73,
    74, 92; October 30
ekkyklema 100
Erdman, Nikolai 39
étude 26, 38, 42, 67–9, 71, 73,
    105–6, 111–12, 117, 126–50,
    153
expressiveness 19, 76, 115, 126,
    143
Eyre, Richard 81

Fellowship of the New Drama 8–9
formalism 41

Gan, Aleksei 34
Garin, Erast 60–1, 67, 97–9,
    103–4, 149, 154
Gastev, Aleksei 70
GEKTEMAS 38
GITIS 38
Gladkov, Aleksandr 44
Gnesin, Mikhail 55, 68
Gogol, Nikolai 9, 25, 27, 39, 77–9,
    81–96, 99, 101, 103–5, 108–9;
    'Advice To Those Who Would
    Play The Government Inspector'
    87–8; Gamblers 81, 90; Government
    Inspector 25, 29, 38, 41, 56, 60,
    68, 74, 77–109, 150; Marriage 81
Golovin, Aleksandr 22, 27

Gordon, Mel 149
Goya, Francisco 62, 65–7; Sleep of
    Reason Produces Monsters 66
Gozzi, Carlo 70
Griboedov, Aleksandr 39; Woe to
    Wit 39
Griboedov Prize 5
Grigoriev, Boris 24
grotesque 20, 25, 27, 46, 60–8, 75,
    85, 89, 91, 108–9, 148, 150,
    152
GVYRM 38
GVYTM 38

Hauptmann, Georg 8–10; Before
    Sunrise 8
Hoffmann, E.T.A. 23, 62–5,
    102–4, 108; Adventures on New
    Year's Eve 63; Mines at Falun, 64;
    Sandman 103
Hoover, Marjorie 27
Houghton, Norris 56, 92, 98

Ibsen, Henrik 10, 12–14, 50, 53;
    Doll's House 50–3; Hedda Gabler
    13–14, 53
Ilinsky, Igor 56–7, 97
Imperial Theatres 12, 21–3, 27, 29,
    55, 63, 83

Keaton, Buster 102, 116
Kerensky, Aleksandr 30
Keystone Cops 37, 103
kinetic staging 29, 100
Kiselyov, Victor 99
Knipper, Olga 6
Komissarzhevskaya, Vera 12–14,
    16, 21, 25, 52, 62
Komissarzhevsky, Fedor 12
Kosheverov, Aleksandr 8
Kustov, Nikolai 42, 149–50
Kuzmin, Mikhail 21

Law, Alma 37, 149
Leach, Robert 8, 39, 75, 149
Lenin, Vladimir 39, 44
Lermontov, Mikhail 27; *Masquerade* 27–9, 39
Levinski, Aleksei 42, 117, 126–7, 138, 142, 149–50
Love of Three Oranges 26
Lunacharsky, Anatoly 30, 37–8, 95

Maeterlinck, Maurice 9–12, 14, 18, 26; *Death of Tintagiles* 10–11, 14; *Sister Beatrice* 12, 14–17
Marinetti, Filippo 69, 86
Marinsky Theatre 23
mask 19, 46, 57–62, 76, 78, 119
MAT *see* Moscow Art Theatre
Mayakovsky, Vladimir 30, 32, 38–9; *Bathhouse* 30; *Bedbug* 29–30; *Mystery Bouffe* 29–30, 32, 38
Ma, Yo-Yo 97
Mendelyeva, Lyubov 17
Meyerhold, Alvina 4
Meyerhold, Emil 4
Meyerhold Theatre, The 37–9, 41–109
Mime Centrum 141
Mingus, Charlie 145
montage 46, 60, 73–6, 91–2, 95, 109, 152
Moscow Art Theatre 5–6, 8–9, 12–13, 22, 38, 44, 47–9
Mulrine, Steven 96
musicality 4, 11, 14, 21, 26, 50, 57, 91, 95, 99

National Theatre 81
Naturalism 8–10, 13–14, 18–19, 46–9, 51–2, 60, 75, 153
Nemirovich-Danchenko, Vladimir 4–6, 9–10, 22

Now I Should Laugh, If I Were Not Dead 150–2

Ostrovsky, Aleksandr 9, 39
otkaz 55–7, 106, 115, 120, 123–5, 127, 138–41, 144, 147

passive 127, 131, 133–4, 144–5, 153; *see also* active
Pavlov, Ivan 9, 32–3, 71–3; *see also* reflexology
playfulness 26, 34, 57, 73, 112, 116, 125, 143–4, 146
Poe, Lugné; *see* Théâtre de l'Œuvre
Popova, Lyubov 9, 34, 37
Popular Theatre 17–18, 21, 23, 26–7, 32, 54, 58–9, 73,
posil' 55–7, 106, 115, 120, 123–4, 127, 138–40, 143, 147, 153
precision 19, 70, 76, 112–13, 120, 122, 125–6, 142, 146
Pushkin, Aleksandr 82, 86

Realism 82
reflexology 71
responsiveness 105, 112, 116, 122, 125–6, 144
Revolution, The 1–3, 9, 23, 26, 29–32, 41, 45, 59, 68–9, 71
rhythm 16, 19, 26, 46, 48–50, 52–7, 68, 70–1, 73, 75–6, 91–2, 95, 98–100, 103–6, 108, 112, 113, 115, 120–7, 138–48, 152–3
RSFSR Theatre 38
Rudnitsky, Konstantin 25, 79
Russian Academy of Theatrical Art 38

Sapunov, Nikolai 11, 21, 25
Savarese, Nicola 149
Schmidt, Paul 97, 99, 149

Schnitzler, Arthur: *Columbine's Scarf* 25

Schuler, Catherine 13

Shakespeare, William 26, 69–70; *Merchant of Venice* 9; *Midsummer Night's Dream* 9; *Othello* 69, 86

Shchepkin, Mikhail 81

Shostakovitch, Dmitri 55

Socialist Realism 41

Sohn Theatre 38

Solovyov, Vladimir 25–6, 68; *Harlequin the Marriage Broker* 25

Stalin, Joseph 2, 39, 42, 44, 82

Stanislavsky, Konstantin 2–3, 5–6, 8–12, 19, 22, 26, 41, 44, 47, 49, 81, 91–2; *An Actor's Work on Himself* 44; *My Life in Art* 9; *see also* System

Stepanova, Varvara 9, 37

Strindberg, August: *Miss Julie* 10

stylisation 10, 21, 46, 50–3, 60, 75, 152

Sudeikin, Sergei 11

Sukhovo-Kobylin, Aleksandr 37, 39; *Death of Tarelkin* 29, 37

Symbolism 8, 10, 18, 23, 62

Symons, James M. 34

System, the 6, 19, 26

Taylor, Frederick Winslow 32–3, 70, 73; *see also* Taylorism

Taylorism 32, 70

Telyakovsky, Vladimir 22

TEO 30, 37

Théâtre d'Art 10

Théâtre Libre 10

Théâtre de l'Œuvre 10

Theatre of Satire 42

Theatre Studio 10–11, 13–14

tochka 55–7, 106, 115, 120, 123–5, 127, 138–40, 143, 147

Tolstoy, Aleksei: *Tsar Fyodor Ivanovitch* 6

Tovstonogov, Georgi 81

Trotsky, Leon 42

Tsar Nicholas I 82

Tsar Nicholas II 44

Turgenev, Ivan 82–3

Urbanovich, P. 149

Verdi, Giuseppe: *Rigoletto* 41

Verhaeren, Émile: *Dawn* 38

Volkov, Nikolai 13, 25

Wagner, Richard 55

Worral, Nick 104

Zarilli, Phillip 149

Zhdanov, Andrei 41

Zola, Émile 9

eBooks – at www.eBookstore.tandf.co.uk

A library at your fingertips!

eBooks are electronic versions of printed books. You can store them on your PC/laptop or browse them online.

They have advantages for anyone needing rapid access to a wide variety of published, copyright information.

eBooks can help your research by enabling you to bookmark chapters, annotate text and use instant searches to find specific words or phrases. Several eBook files would fit on even a small laptop or PDA.

NEW: Save money by eSubscribing: cheap, online access to any eBook for as long as you need it.

Annual subscription packages

We now offer special low-cost bulk subscriptions to packages of eBooks in certain subject areas. These are available to libraries or to individuals.

For more information please contact
webmaster.ebooks@tandf.co.uk

We're continually developing the eBook concept, so keep up to date by visiting the website.

www.eBookstore.tandf.co.uk